COUNTY TRAINING SCHOOLS
AND
PUBLIC SECONDARY EDUCATION
FOR NEGROES IN THE SOUTH

County Training Schools
and
Public Secondary Education
For Negroes in the South

EDWARD E. REDCAY

Submitted in Partial Fulfillment of the Requirements for
the Degree of Doctor of Philosophy in
the Faculty of Philosophy,
Columbia University
1935

NEGRO UNIVERSITIES PRESS
WESTPORT, CONNECTICUT

Originally published in 1935
by The John F. Slater Fund, Washington, D.C.

Reprinted in 1970 by
Negro Universities Press
A Division of Greenwood Press, Inc.
Westport, Connecticut

Library of Congress Catalogue Card Number 72-106864

SBN 8371-3486-2

Printed in the United States of America

Foreword

Every tenth resident of the United States is a person of African descent. Our twelve million Negroes, in other words, constitute one tenth of the total population. Of the 31,500,000 children 5 to 17 years of age in our population, almost 3,000,000 or another 10 per cent are colored. Proportionate comparisons end here, however, for as commonly known, these three million children of the Negro race suffer most unfortunate discrimination. Their school terms average 2 months less than the white school year; attendance is difficult and irregular; enrollment is congested in the first three grades; buildings are dilapidated and inaccessible; and teaching equipment is meagre or lacking. Even more serious is the instructional situation under which large numbers of unqualified teachers are still retained and paid salaries averaging less than half of the white school salaries. Dominating all else is the problem of financial support, involving a current annual expenditure of $87.22 per child for the United States as a whole but an annual expenditure of only $12.57 for the average Negro child.

Notwithstanding the discrimination cited above, amazing progress has been made in all phases of Negro education during the last twenty years. Nor is this a problem of the South alone. Two million Negroes now live outside the South with thousands more moving North annually. Moreover, the South could not possibly meet the situation adequately, even though inclined to do so, since the per capita wealth of this region in 1930 was only $1,785 as compared with $3,080 for the country as a whole, and $3,609 for the North and West or Non-South. Rather is the issue one of national responsibility, significant to the North as well as to the South, and to be solved only through Federal participation and financial aid.

The development of any race depends upon its leadership, and leadership, in turn, is dependent upon advanced education. This at once establishes the importance of secondary education for Negroes and reveals the significance of the *County Training School* which, as shown in this study, was the early fore-runner of the Negro high school.

The John F. Slater Fund, under which County Training Schools have been promoted, was the first educational foundation in the United States to be devoted wholly to the education of Negroes. Being first in the field it has naturally developed pioneer characteristics and has worked out a number of basic principles adopted later by other philanthropic agencies. One of these has been the principle of building on the basis of reality and of meeting people and conditions where they were at the time of contact. Twenty or more years ago when the Slater Fund became interested in public secondary education for Negroes public opinion in the South would hardly have tolerated the idea of secondary education for Negroes. It was quite willing, however, to embrace the suggestion of *industrialized* schools in which the Negro youth of the period might be *trained* for greater efficiency in farming, home-making and teaching. To develop these self-same schools years later into full-fledged high schools became a comparatively easy task.

Another basic principle of Slater Fund policy, widely adopted since by later foundations, has been the splendid cooperation induced through its aid. County Training Schools, in general, throughout the years of their existence have been supported only in part by Slater funds, much of the remaining cost being advanced by public school officials from local revenues. This has proved a most influential force in stimulating the interest and in the changing of attitudes of those responsible for the distribution of public money.

With such a record of history and achievement it is most appropriate that the activity of this oldest foundation in the Negro secondary school field should be studied and evaluated at this time for its own future guidance, as well as for the many fruitful suggestions it has to offer other agencies. It is fitting, also, that this study should be made by a young man somewhat detached from the scene of action, yet close enough to those who waged the struggle to catch something of their spirit and enthusiasm for the conquest. Such a chronicler is Mr. Edward E. Redcay, who has undertaken the present account and who seems admirably qualified for this task in both temperament and background; qualified in background because of his experience and close associations during the past several years with President Arthur D. Wright of the Slater Fund; and qualified in temperament because of his devoted adherence to the ideals and methods of democratic human relationship.

Foreword

These basic qualifications Mr. Redcay has re-enforced further with two years of extensive research in the field, during which time he has visited in person over a third of the county training schools now in operation.

The report thus presented by Mr. Redcay is not only the first historical presentation of Slater Fund activity in this field, but also the most complete analysis of the Negro secondary school situation since the epoch-making study by Dr. Thomas Jesse Jones of the Phelps Stokes Fund in 1915. Among the significant findings of the inquiry, to which those responsible for the development of Negro secondary education should give attention, are the following:

1. There has been amazing growth in secondary education in general during the period of this investigation. In the Negro aspects of this growth the Slater Fund has exerted profound influence. Notwithstanding this progress, however, in 1933 there were still 190 counties in the South entirely without public secondary facilities for Negroes.
2. Public high schools for Negroes are *small* and because of this smallness require special adaptation and modification of general secondary school procedure.
3. Negro children in rural areas do not yet share the same opportunity for secondary education as that afforded the Negro child in urban centers.

The recommendations with which the study concludes are worthy of careful consideration, especially the proposal looking to the establishment of experimental rural high schools for Negroes in each of the Southern States.

In brief, students of education will find in this treatment of the Slater Fund, and particularly in the wise and far-reaching leadership of Dr. James Hardy Dillard, as reflected in this movement, a most suggestive example of sound educational practice. To all such, and to others concerned more generally with the whole intricate question of American race relations, this volume is heartily commended.

MABEL CARNEY.

Teachers College,
Columbia University,
New York City.

ACKNOWLEDGMENTS

A study such as this is possible only when many persons cooperate. Not less than two thousand city, county, and state educational administrators have given aid. The cooperation of the State Agents for Negro Education in the Southern states was particularly valuable. To all these persons the author is indebted.

Appreciative acknowledgment is made of the constructive criticism given by Dr. F. W. Cyr, Dr. W. S. Elsbree, and Dr. E. K. Fretwell.

The greatest indebtedness is to Professor Mabel Carney, and to President Arthur D. Wright of the John F. Slater Fund, without whose sustained interest and assistance this study would have been impossible.

If this work possesses merit, it is by reason of the cooperation of those who have contributed in ways too numerous to mention.

E. R.

Contents

CHAPTER	PAGE
Foreword	vii

I. Introduction 1
    Historical Background 1
    The Growth of Public Secondary Education for
        Negroes 2
    The Purpose of this Investigation 8
    Methods Employed and Sources of Data 9
    Definition of Terms 12
    Digest of Literature Relative to the Investigation ... 14
    Summary 23

II. The Development of County Training Schools
    in the South 24
    The Beginning of the County Training School
        Movement 24
    Policies Effective in County Training School Establishment 31
    Aims and Purposes of County Training Schools 33
    Teacher-Training in County Training Schools 37
    Growth of the County Training School Movement 39
    Characteristics of County Training Schools 45

III. The Present Status of Public Secondary Education for Negroes 51
    The Negro Population in the Southern States 51
    The Number of Schools 51
    The Accredited Secondary Schools 54
    The Secondary Enrollment 57
    The Size of Negro Secondary Schools 60
    The Instructional Staff 63
    Organization of Public Secondary Schools for Negroes 65
    Public Secondary Educational Provision for Negroes by Counties 68

IV. The Place of County Training Schools in the
    Public Negro Secondary Field 74
    The County Training Schools Aided by the Slater
        Fund in 1932-33 74
    County Training Schools: Past and Present 75
    County Training Schools and Public Secondary
        Educational Provision for Negroes 83
    State Recognition of County Training Schools 91

CHAPTER	PAGE
V. SUMMARY AND INTERPRETATION	95
The Development of County Training Schools for Negroes	95
The Present Status of Public Secondary Education for Negroes	97
Public Secondary Educational Provision for Negroes in the South by Counties	103
The Place of County Training Schools in the Public Negro Secondary Field	107
County Training Schools and Public Secondary Educational Provision for Negroes	111
Recommendations	114
BIBLIOGRAPHY	117
APPENDIXES	125

Tables

NUMBER		PAGE
I.	Distribution of Schools, Teachers, and Pupils Enrolled in Public Secondary Schools for Negroes in the Southern States in 1915-16	15
II.	Distribution of County Training Schools in Fifteen Southern States as Aided by the John F. Slater Fund Each Year from 1911 to 1932, Inclusive	40
III.	Number of County Training Schools, Teachers, and Secondary Enrollment in County Training Schools, 1912 to 1930	42
IV.	Number of Teachers and Enrollment, and Teachers Salaries in 23 County Training Schools in Ten Southern States. For 1917-18 and 1932-33	43
V.	Public Secondary Schools for Negroes in Seventeen Southern States and the District of Columbia, 1932-33, Classified According to Rural and Urban Distribution	52
VI.	Distribution of Schools According to Number of Years of Secondary Work Offered	53
VII.	Proportion of Schools by Years of Secondary Work Offered Located in Rural and Urban Communities	54
VIII.	Number of Schools, Enrollment and Number of Teachers in Public Secondary Schools for Negroes in Seventeen Southern States and the District of Columbia, 1932-1933	57
IX.	Public Negro Secondary School Enrollment by Years in Seventeen Southern States and the District of Columbia, 1932-1933	58
X.	Percentage of Negroes 15 to 19 Years of Age Enrolled in Public Secondary Schools in 1932-1933	59
XI.	Distribution of Public Secondary Schools for Negroes in Seventeen Southern States and the District of Columbia, 1932-1933, According to Size of Enrollment	60
XII.	Proportion of Each Size Group Located in Rural and Urban Communities	61
XIII.	Distribution of Public Secondary Schools for Negroes in Seventeen Southern States and the District of Columbia, According to Enrollment, 1932-1933	61
XIV.	Number of Teachers and Average Teaching Staff as Found in Four Types of Public Secondary Schools for Negroes in Seventeen Southern States and the District of Columbia, 1932-1933	63
XV.	Number of Counties and the Negro Population 15 to 19 Years of Age in Seventeen Southern States	69
XVI.	Public Secondary School Work for Negroes Offered by Counties in Seventeen Southern States in 1932-1933	71
XVII.	Percentage of Negro Population 15 to 19 Years of Age Living in Counties Offering Less Than Four Years of Secondary Work and the Average Number Per County	72
XVIII.	Secondary Enrollment, Number of Teachers, and Number of County Training Schools Aided by the John F. Slater Fund in 1932-1933	75

NUMBER		PAGE
XIX.	Distribution of County Training Schools in Fifteen Southern States, 1911-1933	76
XX.	Distribution of County Training Schools and Non-Slater-Aided Public Secondary Schools as to Location and Years of Work Offered	78
XXI.	Enrollment in County Training School Group and Non-Slater-Aided Public Secondary Schools for Negroes in Seventeen Southern States, 1932-1933	80
XXII.	Size of Schools Included in the County Training School Group and the Non-Slater-Aided Public Secondary Schools for Negroes in the South	81
XXIII.	The Average Number of Teachers Per School in the County Training School Group and the Non-Slater-Aided Public Secondary Schools for Negroes in the South	82
XXIV.	Counties in Fifteen Southern States Wherein County Training Schools Provide the *Only* Public Secondary Work and Other Counties Wherein These Schools Offer the *Most Advanced* Public Secondary Work	84
XXV.	Relation of Negro Population 15 to 19 Years of Age, in Fifteen Southern States to (a) Per Cent Enrolled in Public Secondary Schools for Negroes; (b) Per Cent Living in Counties Wherein County Training Schools Provide the *Only*, or *Most Advanced*, Secondary Work	86

Tables in Appendixes

APPENDIX B 128

    Tables 1 to 4 Inclusive: Enrollment and Number of Teachers in Rural and Urban 1-Year, 2-Year, 3-Year and 4-Year Public Secondary Schools for Negroes in Seventeen Southern States and the District of Columbia, 1932-1933.

APPENDIX C 130

    Tables 1 to 35 Inclusive: Number of Schools by Years of Work Offered, Enrollment and Number of Teachers in Schools by Years of Work Offered, Counties Offering 0 to 4 years of Public Secondary Work, and the Per Cent of the Negro Population 15 to 19 Years in a State Living in Counties Offering 0 to 4 Years of Secondary Work, —for Each of the Seventeen Southern States.

APPENDIX D 165

    Tables 1 to 4 Inclusive: Enrollment and Number of Teachers in Rural and Urban 1-Year, 2-Year, 3-Year and 4-Year County Training Schools in the South, 1933.

Tables xvii

APPENDIX E ———————————————————————————— 167
Table: Disbursements Made to Public Negro Secondary Schools in Fifteen Southern States Through the John F. Slater Fund, 1911-1933.

Illustrations

PAGE

Reproduction of a Letter Pertaining to the Beginning of the County Training School Movement for Negroes in the South ———————————————————————————— 28
Reproduction of a Printed Form Used by A. M. Strange Who Helped to Establish the First Parish Training School in Louisiana ———————————————————————————— 29
Figure 1. Expenditures for Salaries in County Training Schools as Disbursed Through the John F. Slater Fund and from Public Tax Funds ———————————————————————————— 34
Reproduction of a Bulletin Sent Out by Dr. James Hardy Dillard Pertaining to the Establishment of County Training Schools ———————————————————————————— 36
Figure 2. Distribution of County Training Schools Aided by the John F. Slater Fund, 1911 to 1933, Inclusive———— 76

COUNTY TRAINING SCHOOLS
AND
PUBLIC SECONDARY EDUCATION
FOR NEGROES IN THE SOUTH

Chapter I

INTRODUCTION

HISTORICAL BACKGROUND

PRIOR to the Civil War, few Negroes were offered the opportunity of attending any public school. In several non-slave-holding states in the North they were permitted to attend public schools along with white children, but relatively few Negroes resided in the North and, consequently, only a few children took advantage of the privilege of education at public expense. Of those who did attend few reached the secondary school.[1]

In the slave-holding states of the South during the same period public schools for white children were very slow in developing. Public schools for Negroes virtually were non-existent, and in certain states formal education for Negroes, directly or by implication, was forbidden by law. So it was that the educational opportunities for children of this minority race were only those to be found in the scattered private schools for Negroes, most of which were subsidized and administered by Northern religious and philanthropic organizations. Educational opportunities in these schools rarely extended above the elementary grades and enrollments were very small.[2]

Shortly after the close of the War between the States, the Federal government took the initiative in stimulating the development of schools for Negroes in the South. Through the activity of the Freedmen's Bureau the government literally introduced the idea of elementary schools for Negroes in the Southern states. Private organizations and individuals of both races actively participated in establishing schools during this early Reconstruction period. By 1875 the Southern states had revised their constitutions to conform to the 14th and 15th Amendments to the Constitution and to the Reconstruction Acts of Congress.[3] Thus, along with legal recognition as free indi-

---

[1]Woodson, Carter G. *The Education of the Negro Prior to 1861.* G. P. Putnam's Sons, New York, 1915, pp. 81-120.
[2]Ibid., pp. 205; 151-178.
[3]Long, H. M. *Public Secondary Education for Negroes in North Carolina.* Bureau of Publications, Teachers College, Columbia University, New York, pp. 1-3.

viduals, the Negro began to enjoy one of the most cherished privileges of American citizenship—the opportunity to secure an education at public expense.

Despite the handicaps of racial prejudice, misguided reformers and philanthropists, sectional misunderstandings, adverse political conditions, and other limiting factors, great progress has been made during the last sixty years. The period of development preceding 1900 was characterized by the gradual acceptance of the idea of public schools for Negroes . This, in turn, tended to strengthen the ideal of public schools for *all* children in the South. Perhaps the most important gain during this period was the gradual recognition of the fact that education for individuals of both races was mutually desirable and advantageous for broader social development.

THE GROWTH OF PUBLIC SECONDARY EDUCATION FOR NEGROES

The development of public elementary schools for Negroes throughout the South preceded a similar development of secondary schools. The exact number of public Negro secondary schools which were in existence before 1900 is not known. In 1916, however, Jones[4] reported that there were 64 public high schools for Negroes in the Southern states of which 45 offered four year courses. According to the National Survey of Secondary Education, there were 1,150 public secondary schools for Negroes in 1930. This indicates a tremendous advance in this field of education.

Undoubtedly many factors have contributed to this growth. The popularization and development of public secondary education in the United States as a whole must have been such a factor. According to the United States Office of Education, 11,680 public secondary schools in this country enrolled 1,329,000 pupils in 1916. Ten years later the number of schools had doubled and the enrollment increased three-fold. Considering public Negro secondary schools separately, it is known that in 1916 there were in 15 Southern states 64 public secondary schools enrolling 8,565 pupils.[5] Data are not available for an interval of ten years. Fifteen years later, however, the num-

---

[4]Jones, Thomas Jesse. *Negro Education: A Study of Private and Higher Schools for Colored People in the United States.* United States Bureau of Education Bulletin, 1916, No. 38, Government Printing Office, Washington, D. C., pp. 41-43.
[5]Ibid., p. 42.

ber of schools indicated a 25 to 1 increase, while the enrollment was 12 times that of 1916. From these figures it appears that the amazing growth of public Negro secondary education is not solely attributable to the general expansion of secondary education in the United States.

Certainly the remarkable progress the Negro race has made in other than educational fields since 1865, and particularly since just before the World War, has been a contributing factor.[6] Much of this progress has been due to the Negroes themselves—to their own aspiration and initiative.

The growth of interracial cooperative endeavor must also be considered. It shows a determined advance since 1912. In that year the *Southern Sociological Congress*,[7] by establishing an interracial section, made possible the bringing together of representatives of both races *in the South*. In the same year the *University Commission*[8] was formed for the purpose of interesting college people, particularly those of the white race, in interracial cooperation. Growing out of these efforts emerged the well organized *Commission for Interracial Cooperation*,[9] an organization whose efforts are almost solely devoted to the adjustment of racial groups in economic, political, social and educational affairs.

Then, too, the activity of religious bodies in promoting education for the Negro must have had some effect in quickening both secondary and collegiate educational development. Among the most active of these organizations might be mentioned the several *Methodist Boards,* the *Baptist Associations,* as well as the *American Baptist Home Missions Board* and the *American Missionary Association of the Congregational Churches.*[10] Undoubtedly the independent Negro religious demominations rendered splendid service to the education of the race by establishing schools and colleges.[11] The extent of the activity of religious

---

[6]Work, Monroe N. *The Negro Year Book, 1931-32.* The Negro Year Book Publishing Company, Tuskegee, Alabama, pp. 118-122.
[7]The Phelps-Stokes Fund. *Twenty Year Report of the Phelps-Stokes Fund, 1911-1931.* The Phelps-Stokes Fund, 1932, Office: 101 Park Avenue, New York City, p. 57.
[8]Ibid., p. 54.
[9]Ibid., p. 54.
[10]Holmes, D. O. W. *The Evolution of the Negro College.* Bureau of Publications, Teachers College, Columbia University, New York City, pp. 67-137.
[11]Ibid., pp. 138-149.

groups is evident when it is pointed out that of 117 privately and publicly supported institutions offering higher education for Negro youth in 1933, 72 were under the control of some religious group.

More important than the activity of these bodies, however, is the rapid development in Negro higher education which has taken place since 1916. Of 92,593 students enrolled in institutions reputed to be of collegiate rank in 1916, only 2,641, or less than 2 per cent, were of college grade.[12] In 1933 the total enrollment in 110 institutions offering higher education for Negroes had fallen to 54,163 students, but the number enrolled for work of college grade jumped to 38,274, or 71 per cent of the total.[13] Educational advances and opportunities at the top most certainly exert some upward pull upon the lower levels. In this sense, this rapid growth in higher institutions of learning has played a part in the development of public Negro secondary facilities.

While the statistics are not easily segregated in order to indicate the contribution to the advancement in Negro education, it is certain that funds made available through such Federal legislation as the Morrill Act, the Smith-Hughes Act, and the Authorizing Act for Howard University, may have contributed indirectly.

Another factor which must be considered pertains to the activity of the philanthropic agencies in the field of Negro education. The activity of the Educational Funds is particularly important. With the exception of the Slater Fund, those most interested in improving educational facilities for the minority race have originated during the early years of the period marking the rapid growth in this field.

Two of these Funds were specifically originated to aid the Negro's educational advancement. The John F. Slater Fund dates back to 1882.[14] Before 1911 this Fund applied its major efforts to colleges for Negroes, and most of its activity centered

---
[12]Ibid., pp. 159.
[13]The John F. Slater Fund. *Proceedings and Reports*, For Year Ending June 30, 1934, pp. 16-21.
[14]Trustees of the John F. Slater Fund. *Documents Relating to the Origin and Work of the Slater Fund and Work of the Slater Trustees*. Occasional Papers, No. 1, 1894, pp. 9-10.

Introduction 5

around the improvement of teaching by increasing salaries and enabling teachers to receive better preparation. After 1911 the emphasis of this Fund shifted to the stimulation and development of public secondary school facilities. The Negro Rural School Fund, Inc. (Anna T. Jeanes Foundation) was established in 1907 and devotes its resources entirely to the improvement of small rural schools for Negroes, by cooperating with public school authorities in providing trained supervisors for these schools.[15] Both of these Funds are administered under one executive and field staff, although they have separate Boards.

The interest of Julius Rosenwald in Negro education dates from 1912, and a large proportion of his personal philanthropy has gone to Negro education.[16] The Fund bearing his name was reorganized in 1928, and a larger and more varied program of assistance and stimulation in the interest of rural Negro education has been put into effect.[17] This Fund has exerted wide-spread influence for the provision of better physical plants for Negro schools in that it has participated in almost 6,000 building projects in Negro education, most of which have been in the elementary field. Since 1928 its administrators have aided also in the enlargement of libraries, the extension of school terms, and in giving special assistance to counties where no Rosenwald schools had been constructed previously.

The Phelps-Stokes Fund, established in 1911, has made direct appropriations to schools, acted as a source and a disseminator of Negro educational information, and at critical times has augmented the resources and activity of other groups working in this field.[18]

The General Education Board[19] was incorporated in 1903. While the activities of this Board are applied without distinction of race, it has directed its efforts chiefly toward higher education, and all education in the South. The aid rendered Negro education in the South has been used to help private in-

[15] Wright, Arthur D. *The Negro Rural School Fund, Inc.* (The Anna T. Jeanes Foundation), Published by The Negro Rural School Fund, Inc., Washington, D. C., 1933, pp. 1-10.
[16] Leavell, Ullin W. *Philanthropy in Negro Education.* Cullom and Ghertner Co., Nashville, Tenn., 1930, pp. 76-78.
[17] Ibid., p. 79.
[18] The Phelps-Stokes Fund. op. cit., pp. 3-31.
[19] The General Education Board. *Report*, 1902-1914, p. 3-14.

stitutions established by Northern church organizations and Southern Negroes, and in cooperatively stimulating the development of an efficient system of public education for Negroes in the South. In the field of higher education the General Education Board has acquired considerable authority and influence through its own research and staff organizations. In the elementary and secondary fields of Negro education this Board has always contributed large sums toward the projects of other philanthropic Funds directly interested in these divisions. The distribution of these sums has been left, usually, to the administrative personnel of the Fund directly interested in the specific field or project. One of the most potent influences apparently related to the rapid growth in public Negro education resulted from the willingness of the General Education Board to take up the task of supporting the State Agents for Negro Education as members of the staff of State Superintendents of Education in the Southern states. These agents stand as the pivotal men in relation to Negro educational development in their respective states.

In the past, two additional philanthropic agencies have aided this field of education. The Carnegie Corporation has, from time to time, augmented the resources of the several Funds by specific grants.[20] The Peabody Education Fund was founded in 1867 to aid the more destitute portions of the Southern and Southwestern states. The philanthropy of this Fund was applied to both races, and it is difficult to segregate that which was specifically allocated to Negro education. It was at the request of this Fund that the General Education Board took over the support of the State Agents in 1911. The definite interest of this Fund in Negro education is indicated by the final distribution of the Fund in 1914 after 46 years' activity. At that time it made a gift to the Slater Board of $350,000, because the latter Fund was devoted solely to Negro education.[21]

Not only has there been great progress in Negro education, but during the last 30 years the general educational develop-

[20] The John F. Slater Fund. *Proceedings and Reports*, For Year Ending September 30, 1930, p. 6.
[21] Leavell, Ullin W. op. cit., pp. 59; 83-94.

Introduction

ment of the South has improved tremendously. Knight has this to say,

"Measured by its own record . . . the educational progress of the South since 1900 has been remarkable . . . Measured by its needs and by national standards, however, the South is not yet an educationally advanced section of the country. The Southern State which has made the greatest progress should do twice as much as it now does for the maintenance of its schools in order to rank educationally even as an *average* State among the forty-eight—a place to which not a single Southern State has yet attained."[22]

In concluding this discussion of factors which contributed to the tremendous growth in public secondary education for Negroes, this remains to be said. Factors which contributed to the growth of *all* secondary education in the United States, directly or indirectly, are related to the specific growth in the Negro field. These factors are undoubtedly both numerous and difficult of analysis. Probably more important than any factors mentioned is that which is concerned with the increasing willingness of the public, both lay and professional, to support and administer Negro educational agencies. Stimulative appropriations from philanthropic and Federal funds have been dwarfed by the sums derived from public tax sources, a fact which is carefully pointed out in another chapter of this study. After all, the remarkable growth has been in *public* secondary education. Perhaps the most valuable thought for all interested in the education of persons, regardless of race, color or creed, is that we have seen in Negro education evidence to support the belief that white and colored persons, local, state and federal governments, religious organizations and philanthropy have employed and possibly learned the value of *cooperative* endeavor.

Prior to the present study little or no attempt had been made to present the historical facts pertaining to this development. Consequently, there is need for an investigation of the factors or agencies particularly involved in this great advance in Negro education, about which there is available information. It is with one of these factors or agencies that the present study is concerned. So it is that the following quotation marks the point of departure for this investigation:

[22]Knight, Edgar W. *Education in the United States.* Ginn and Company, Boston, New York, etc., 1929, pp. 489-490.

". . . in 1911 when *County Training Schools*[23] were first established there were no rural high schools for Negroes in the South and very few in the cities."[24]

THE PURPOSE OF THIS INVESTIGATION

As early as 1910 Dr. James Hardy Dillard, the general agent of the John F. Slater Fund, became interested in the task of providing public secondary facilities for Negroes in the South. At that time the movement to provide such education was in its infancy. Largely through his leadership the Slater Fund committed itself to a policy of encouraging the establishment and development of public Negro secondary schools in county systems of schools. The major activity of the Fund has centered in cooperating financially with local agencies willing to share in the initial expenditures as well as continuing support of such educational undertakings; and in encouraging the establishment of *County Training Schools* as a type of secondary school planned to meet the needs of a Negro population largely rural. During the last 22 years the constructive and stimulative efforts of this philanthropy were applied in 612 such schools located in 517 counties in 15 Southern states maintaining separate schools for the races.

The purpose of this investigation is to study and present the facts and circumstances surrounding the establishment and development of these County Training Schools for Negroes. An attempt will be made to determine the extent to which this movement in public Negro secondary education has developed along lines indicated by the objectives and policies set forth by those agencies instrumental in sponsoring it. An endeavor, also, will be made to determine to what extent these schools may be considered a significant part of the public Negro secondary field as it exists today.

On the basis of the facts presented it is hoped that possible

---

[23]The author was unable to secure conclusive data pertaining to the origin of the term, *County Training School*. However, as is pointed out in detail in Chapter II, these schools from the beginning were to be centrally located schools open to all Negro children in a *county*. They were expected to supply the rural elementary schools with better *trained* teachers than were generally available when the schools were started, and they were encouraged to offer "industrial training, laying particular emphasis upon subjects pertaining to home and farm." It is possible that the name associated with the schools evolved from their functional nature as conceived by the persons who sponsored them.

[24]Newbold, N. C. "Common Schools for Negroes in the South." *The Annals of the American Academy of Political and Social Science*, Vol. CXXXX, 1928, p. 220.

procedures and principles may be suggested to aid in the future development of public secondary educational opportunities for children of this minority race.

METHODS EMPLOYED AND SOURCES OF DATA

One phase of the study concerned with those schools known as County Training Schools will involve an investigation of the early beginnings of these schools, the policies effective in their establishment, their growth and the development of aims and functions. This, naturally, must include a consideration of the efforts and methods employed by the Slater Fund to stimulate and raise the level of secondary education for Negroes. An attempt, therefore, will be made to reveal some of the interphilanthropic relations whereby cooperative endeavor was directed toward the development of secondary education.

The method employed for this phase of the study is primarily historical. The data were selected from records, correspondence, statistical and financial reports and audits, and documents written by executive officers of the several philanthropic agencies who participated in the County Training School movement; official printed reports and proceedings of the Slater Fund; contracts of county superintendents of schools; reports of principals of County Training Schools; records, reports, and correspondence from State Agents of Negro Education; reports of State Superintendents of Education and state school laws. These original sources were supplemented by such existing literature as could be considered reliable. Personal interviews with authorities familiar with this development in education also proved helpful in conducting the research.

In order to determine how consistently the County Training School movement had developed in comparison with the objectives actuating those who sponsored it, certain factual data had to be gathered. An analysis was made of the aims, objectives, and policies operative in the establishing and functioning of these schools. In light of the findings it was discovered that the information gathered would have to answer such questions pertaining to status, as follows: How many schools have been identified with the County Training School movement? How are they distributed among the counties of the Southern states? Are they located in rural or urban communities? Are they one-year, two-year, three-year or four-year secondary schools? What is the secondary enrollment by grades? How many full-time and part-time secondary teachers are employed? How many of these schools are accredited? Where are they found?

It follows that this same information would have to be secured from all public schools offering secondary work for Negroes in the South if any indication of the place these Training Schools have in this field is to be revealed. Some questions this portion of the study attempts to answer follow: What proportion of existing public Negro secondary schools is identified with the County Training School movement? How do these schools compare with other Negro schools as to size, rural or urban location, type of school by years of secondary work offered, and accredited standing? What proportion of those enrolled in public Negro secondary schools seek education in Training Schools? In how many counties are the Training Schools the only public schools, or the schools offering the highest secondary grades? What proportion of the potential Negro secondary school population lives in these counties? To what extent do the several states rely upon these schools to provide the secondary educational services for their Negro constituencies?

A logical extension of this phase of the investigation involves an effort to relate certain aspects of the status of existing Negro secondary schools to the number and distribution of the Negro secondary school population found in the geographical areas studied. Such a discussion should be of value when considering the future development and stimulation of public secondary education for Negroes. Some leading questions follow: How many counties with a considerable potential Negro secondary school population are entirely without public secondary schools? How many counties provide some public secondary educational facilities, but less than four years? How many have at least one four-year secondary school? How many counties provide at least one fully accredited four-year secondary school? Where are these counties located? What proportion of the potential Negro secondary school population is enrolled in secondary schools in the counties in the several

Introduction 11

states? What proportion of this potential secondary school population in the different counties, parishes, and states is without public secondary school opportunities? The method employed in treating the several factors of status relative to County Training Schools and all public schools offering secondary work is largely statistical. A preliminary survey of existing data about public Negro secondary education in the South soon indicated that professional educators and research students in this field have been handicapped by a dearth of reliable objective data. Much of the statistical information available regarding secondary education makes no intelligible differentiations with respect to separate schools for the two races. Most specific studies in the field of Negro secondary education have been "sampling" studies. While valuable, they leave the picture incomplete as to actual status.

So it happened that part of this investigation had to be devoted to securing a more complete and reliable body of objective data than was available heretofore. *All statistical tables and data used in this study, unless labelled to the contrary, are drawn from a special inquiry sent to every county, special district, and city superintendent of schools in the seventeen[25] states included in this investigation, and to the State Agents for Negro Education.*

A concise and compact questionnaire[26] was devised to yield the data pertaining to status required for this study and, at the same time, to be of practical use beyond the particular needs of this project. Printed upon cards, and so numbered as to constitute an accurate index, the questionnaires form the basis for a file which lists all public schools offering secondary work for Negroes in the individual counties of the states included in the study.

Owing to the sponsoring of the inquiry by the Slater Fund, which has been functioning in the field of Negro education for 52 years; to a careful and insistent follow-up technique;

---

[25] Alabama, Arkansas, Delaware, Florida, Georgia, Kentucky, Louisiana, Maryland, Mississippi, Missouri, North Carolina, Oklahoma, South Carolina, Tennessee, Texas, Virginia, and West Virginia.

[26] The data secured by the author for this investigation are available in printed form. The John F. Slater Fund, *Public Secondary Schools for Negroes in the Southern States of the United States.* Occasional Papers No. 29, (pp. 72), Washington, D. C., 1935.

See Appendix A for a reproduction of the questionnaire.

and to the energetic cooperation of the State Agents for Negro Education, very complete information was obtained.

In checking the accuracy and completeness of the returns, the following sources were utilized: records and other data in the offices of the State Agents for Negro Education in the several states; annual and biennial reports of State Superintendents of Education; bulletins and pamphlets released by state departments of education; and data from the office of Dr. Ambrose Caliver, Specialist in the Education of Negroes in the United States Office of Education.

Throughout the investigation every effort was made to avoid errors, by checking with as many sources as were available. In nearly all cases where questionnaire data were checked with such records as were usable, the factual data were found accurate to an exceedingly high degree.

To obtain first-hand information concerning the study, seventy County Training Schools and high schools were visited in ten Southern states. Many rural elementary schools and several institutions of higher learning for Negroes were also included in the field trip in order to secure a more comprehensive picture of Negro education. To check data, a visit to the office of the State Agent for Negro Education in the State Department of Education in each state was made. At the same time information was secured to facilitate interpretation of the several phases of the study which demanded particular explanation in view of local and state considerations concerning Negro education.

Additional sources of data utilized in this phase of the investigation were: The United States Census of 1930; pamphlets and bulletins issued by the several states indicating the prevailing standards in accrediting schools; lists of accredited schools and standards employed by regional accrediting agencies; important literature, some of which is reviewed in another section of this chapter; and unpublished data in the offices of the several philanthropic agencies interested in Negro secondary education.

DEFINITION OF TERMS

The term *County Training School,* as used in this study, refers to those larger public county schools for Negroes in

Introduction 13

the Southern states which are open in the higher grades to children from all parts of the county, and offering, or planning to offer, work including the eighth grade or higher, and which have been aided by the John F. Slater Fund. A careful study has revealed that no school for Negroes in the South has been called a County Training School unless it has been aided by this Fund at some time.

For purposes of this study, the term *status* includes the following: number of public secondary schools, number of years of secondary work offered, enrollment in secondary grades,[27] total enrollment in all grades in a school, size of school in terms of enrollment, number of full-time and part-time secondary teachers, number of accredited schools, the distribution of secondary schools by rural or urban location, and the distribution of secondary schools in relation to the number and distribution of the Negro secondary school population in the geographical areas studied.

A school is classified as *rural* if it is found in the open country or in a town or village having a population of less than 2,500 persons. An *urban* school is one found in a town or city of 2,500 or more inhabitants. Sometimes Negro schools are located just outside the ordinary limits of urban centers. These schools can hardly be classed as rural unless adequate transportation facilities are provided. Such factors were carefully considered in making the rural-urban classification of the schools included in this investigation.

In considering the teaching staff of the secondary schools studied, a *part-time teacher* is one who divides his or her time between the elementary grades and secondary subjects. For purposes of comparison such a teacher is considered equal to one-half a full-time teacher.

Throughout the discussion which follows, frequent reference is made to the Negro population between the ages of 15 to 19 years, inclusive. No brief is held that this age group constitutes an entirely satisfactory representation of the actual Negro high school population. It is used as the approximate

[27]In states having the eleven grade (7-4) system, the eighth grade was considered the first year of secondary work; in the twelve grade system the ninth grade was taken as the first year of the secondary school whether in an 8-4, 6-3-3, or 6-6 plan of organization.

or potential secondary group. Since this study involves seventeen states, as well as heterogeneous political and administrative units within given states, a common differential for comparative purposes was needed. Owing to the divergent practices employed by the several states in reporting enumeration, enrollment, and other pertinent data concerning Negro educables, it was found expedient to use the age group nearest to that of Negro secondary pupils reported by counties in the United States Census of 1930.

There is further justification for the use of this age grouping. Dr. Leonard V. Koos, as Associate Director of the National Survey of Secondary Education, approved the use of this differential for that phase of the survey pertaining to Negroes in the Southern states. Dr. Ambrose Caliver contends that these ages are more representative of Negroes attending secondary school than the age group of 14 to 17 inclusive.[28] The use of this age group is further justified by the fact that the typical Negro student entering college is twenty years of age.[29]

The *non-Slater-aided schools* are those which have never been assisted by the Slater Fund as County Training Schools.

DIGEST OF LITERATURE RELATIVE TO THE INVESTIGATION

A brief summary of the studies applicable to this investigation is set forth in the following pages.

There has been but one reasonably complete study of the early status of secondary education for Negroes in the District of Columbia and the Southern states. In 1915 the Phelps-Stokes Fund, in cooperation with the United States Bureau of Education and under the direction of Dr. Thomas Jesse Jones,[30] undertook to supply, through an impartial and thorough investigation, the facts showing the status of Negro education as revealed by an examination of colleges and secondary schools, both private and public. The investigation was undertaken at

---

[28] Caliver, Ambrose. *Secondary Education for Negroes*. United States Bureau of Education Bulletin, 1932, No. 17, Monograph No. 7, Government Printing Office, Washington, D. C. p. 15.
[29] Caliver, Ambrose. *A Background Study of Negro College Students*. United States Bureau of Education Bulletin, 1933, No. 8. Government Printing Office, Washington, D. C. pp. 14, 112.
[30] Jones, Thomas Jesse. *Negro Education: A Study of Private and Higher Schools for Colored People in the United States*. U. S. Bureau of Education Bulletins, 1916, Nos. 38, 39. Government Printing Office, Washington, D. C.

a time when little or nothing definite was known about Negro education in the South as a whole. It serves as a landmark from which we can determine certain aspects of the rapid development of secondary schools for Negro children. The report indicates that in 1916 the District of Columbia and the Southern states, which maintain separate schools for the races possessed 45 public secondary schools offering four year courses and 19 offering three years of high school work. Approximately 8,500 pupils were enrolled in the secondary grades of these schools and were taught by 467 teachers. These schools were all located in urban centers.

TABLE 1

DISTRIBUTION OF SCHOOLS, TEACHERS, AND PUPILS ENROLLED IN PUBLIC SECONDARY SCHOOLS FOR NEGROES IN THE SOUTHERN STATES, IN 1915-16

State	NUMBER OF		
	Schools	Pupils Enrolled	Teachers
Alabama	4	541	19
Arkansas	5	253	22
Delaware	1	60	11
District of Columbia	2	1260	81
Florida	2	78	6
Georgia	1	40	5
Kentucky	9	752	42
Maryland	2	781	42
Mississippi	1	49	3
Missouri	3	1163	61
Oklahoma	5	368	27
South Carolina	1	138	6
Texas	13	1212	63
Tennessee	5	650	25
Virginia	5	1070	38
West Virginia	5	150	16
Totals	64	8565	467

Data taken from the report of Thomas Jesse Jones. *Negro Education: A Study of Private and Higher Schools for Colored People in the United States.* U. S. Bureau of Education Bulletins, 1916, Nos. 38, 39. Government Printing Office, Washington, D. C.

An inspection of Table 1 reveals that the majority of these secondary schools were located in the so-called "border states." Alabama, Florida, Georgia, Mississippi and South Carolina together are represented as having possessed only 9 public secondary schools attended by but 846 pupils. By far the great majority of Negroes inhabited these five states. North Carolina and Louisiana are conspicuous by their absence from the list of states offering public secondary education for Negroes.

The Jones study reports 27 County Training Schools, located in ten states. Practically all of these schools were found in small rural villages or the open country. These schools enrolled 5,751 pupils in the elementary grades and 155 in the secondary grades. Several factors, undoubtedly, account for the low high school enrollment, the chief one being that the inadequacy of the elementary school systems was such that few pupils were prepared to use secondary facilities even when provided.

Another related factor of importance concerns the distribution of these schools by states. Five County Training Schools located in North Carolina and two in Louisiana, while enrolling no secondary pupils at that time, had served to initiate the movement, at least, in the rural public secondary education field for Negroes. The location of seven of these schools in Alabama, Georgia, and South Carolina indicated an attempt to promote secondary education in states where little had been done previously and wherein the Negro population was concentrated and largely rural.

In a study of the development of public schools for Negroes, Newbold[31] was primarily concerned with the evolution of elementary schools. The development of secondary schools from practically non-existence in 1900 to more than 250 in 1928 is shown. The data, however, were complete for only seven states and do not adequately represent the status of public Negro secondary schools at that time. It is obvious that the author did not intend his presentation to be representative of the total situation. Mention is made of the fact that when County Training Schools were started no public rural high

[31]Newbold, N. C. "Common Schools for Negroes," *The Annals of the American Academy of Political and Social Science*, Vol. CXXXX, pp. 209-223. (This volume is devoted entirely to a presentation of facts pertaining to Negro life.)

schools for Negroes were in existence. "The leadership of the Slater Fund, always in cooperation and with the hearty approval of the public school officials, must therefore be credited with hastening the day of secondary education for Negroes."[32]

Dr. Lance G. E. Jones[33] of Oxford University, England, made an extensive tour of the Southern states in 1926-1927 and visited many representative schools and colleges for Negroes. He found great variation in the quality of education offered to Negroes. Vast inequalities existed in the allocation of public monies for schools and the discrimination in favor of white schools was greatest where Negro population seemed densest. Educational provisions in rural communities were invariably more limited and inferior than in urban places.

Jones concludes that the greatest handicap to the secondary schools is the generally inferior, out-moded, and inadequate elementary school system. He found the curricula predominantly academic and generally prescribed by state administrative authorities. Teaching was usually poor, classes large, equipment inadequate, and attendance irregular. This study was not intended to be a systematic survey.

Prior to the present study, the only other investigation of County Training Schools was that made by Leo M. Favrot[34] in 1921. The pertinent facts concerning the 142 County Training Schools in existence at that time are considered. The investigation touched upon the general administration and support of these schools; number, salaries, experience and qualifications of teachers; the curricula; attendance and age grade distribution of pupils; and their achievement in silent reading, arithmetic and English composition.

This study made at a time when secondary education for Negroes was just gathering momentum was aimed primarily at improving the Training Schools. At the same time Favrot was attempting to learn the attitude of both races in the South towards the Training School idea. He concluded that the

[32]Ibid., p. 220.
[33]Jones, Lance G. E. *Negro Schools in the Southern States.* The Clarendon Press, Oxford, England, 1928.
[34]Favrot, Leo M. *County Training Schools for Negroes in the South.* Occasional Papers, No. 23, of the John F. Slater Fund, Charlottesville, Va., 1923.

South was generally receptive to the movement and cognizant of the possibilities of these schools. The work of the schools was found not entirely satisfactory, and many recommendations designed to improve the quality of education were included. The study furnishes the only source for comparative treatment of several aspects of the present investigation, and more specific reference will be made to it in the pages which follow.

In a study of public secondary schools for Negroes in the South, Favrot[35] reports 834 schools, of which 712 are public, doing two years or more of secondary work. There were 63,059 pupils enrolled in these public schools. More than two-thirds of those enrolled were in city schools and the remainder were in rural schools.

Unlike Lance Jones, who found the opposite to be true, Favrot reports that in so far as the number of pupils per teacher affects the teaching in high schools it would appear that the Negro high schools generally are not overcrowded and conditions in this respect are satisfactory for efficient work.[36]

Favrot reported 282 counties in the South with a Negro population of twelve and a half per cent or more of the total population without high school facilities. Approximately one-third of the counties in the South were without secondary facilities for Negroes, either public or private. One-fourth of the Negroes in the South lived in these counties.

In most states secondary enrollments were constantly increasing and teachers were becoming better prepared. Favrot concludes that the greatest difficulty lies in the problem of state aid. When appropriations are made to various counties, whether or not Negroes receive their just share depends upon those in local control. Until states have worked out adequate plans for financing rural high schools from state and county funds, the Negro youth will have to attend high schools wherever the facilities are offered, and that is in the larger centers of wealth.

Robinson[37] made a brief study of the opportunity for pub-

---

[35]Favrot, Leo M. "Some Facts About Negro High Schools and Their Distribution and Development in the Southern States," *High School Quarterly*, Vol. XVII, 1929, pp. 139-154.
[36]Ibid., p. 143.
[37]Robinson, W. A. "Four-Year State Accredited High Schools for Negroes in Seventeen Southern States," *Bulletin of the National Association of Teachers in Colored Schools*, Vol. VII, 1927, pp. 6-10.

Introduction 19

lic education of Negroes in four-year state accredited high schools in seventeen Southern states, and in no state was there an approach to equality as far as provisions for the two races were concerned. In a similar type of investigation made a year later, he[38] found that only two and nine-tenths per cent of the four-year accredited high schools were for Negroes, although these persons constituted twenty-five per cent of the total population of the sixteen states studied. With the exception of three states, high schools for Negroes and whites were accredited on the same basis.

H. L. Trigg,[39] Inspector of Secondary Schools for Negroes in North Carolina, studied the academic preparation of teachers in the accredited secondary schools in his state and, quite surprisingly, reveals that colleges within the state do not supply a sufficient number of teachers to meet the secondary demand. Of the 564 teachers studied, only 32.5 per cent had been trained in institutions in the state.

The most recent significant study of the status of secondary education for Negroes is that presented by Caliver[40] as part of the National Survey of Secondary Education. The data reported are for the school year 1929-1930. An important objective of the study was to ascertain status, yet at the same time to collect and report all evidence possible which would show noteworthy practices. The report contains valuable factual information concerning the organization of schools, the Negro high school staff, the Negro high-school pupil, curricula and extra-curricular offerings, housing and equipment, and the availability of secondary education for Negroes.

The portion of the study of pertinent significance concerns certain aspects of the status and availability of schools. Using the best combination of sources at his disposal, Caliver found that there were 1,150 public schools offering from one to four years of secondary work to Negro pupils in fifteen Southern states. There were enrolled in these schools 101,998 pupils.

---

[38]Robinson, W. A. "Four-Year State Accredited High Schools for Negroes in the South," *Bulletin of the National Association of Teachers in Colored Schools*, Vol. VIII, 1928, pp. 6-15.
[39]Trigg, H. L. "Sources and Comparative Data Relative to the Teaching Staff of North Carolina Accredited Negro High Schools for 1929-1930," *North Carolina Teachers Record*, Vol. 1, 1930, pp. 6-8.
[40]Caliver, Ambrose. *Secondary Education for Negroes*. U. S. Bureau of Education Bulletin, 1932, No. 17, Monograph No. 7, Government Printing Office, Washington, D. C.

Of the total number of schools discovered, 643 were in rural locations. Exactly 200 of these offered four years of secondary work. The remaining 507 schools were located in urban centers, and 306 were four-year secondary schools.

In 1930 there were 230 counties in the South with a considerable Negro high school population entirely without public high school facilities. Approximately 200,000 Negroes of high school age lived in these counties. In addition, Caliver reports 195 counties offering some high school work, but less than four years. More than 160,000 Negro children fifteen to nineteen years of age lived in these counties. It seems that 37 per cent of all Negroes fifteen to nineteen years of age in the South resided in counties offering less than four years of public secondary work.

Referring to County Training Schools, Caliver reports 131 and considers the growth of these schools as one of the most important recent developments in Negro education.[41] Caliver concludes that Negro high schools are in general of recent development and many are inaccessible to the constituency they are intended to serve. Most of these schools began offering a four-year program after 1915, and practically all of the 244 having an accredited status have attained this recognition since 1920. Differences in secondary school facilities between the colored and white races are in most cases evident, and in practically every instance of major importance are in favor of the whites. He concludes that in spite of progress made in secondary education for Negroes, they have a long way to go before the educational chasm between the two races is bridged. Meanwhile the Negro race must continue to face the competition of American life at an enormous disadvantage.

Few state-wide studies of education reveal clear-cut information specifically concerned with Negro education as a whole, —much less with reference to secondary education. Perhaps more accurate information is available concerning Negro education in North Carolina than any other state. Long[42] made a study of secondary education for Negroes in this state. He

[41]Ibid., p. 33.
[42]Long, Hollis Moody. *Public Secondary Education for Negroes in North Carolina*. Bureau of Publications, Teachers College, Columbia University, New York City, 1932.

Introduction 21

found that in no other Southern state has public secondary education for Negroes developed so rapidly. This growth dates from 1918. In 1929 Long found that there were 111 schools offering one to four years of work. Inequalities in provision for educational opportunity were evident, since every county in North Carolina had at least one four-year secondary school for whites, while 32 of the 100 counties were either without public secondary schools for Negroes or provided less than four years of work on the secondary level.

Buildings were, in 85 per cent of the cases, less than ten years old and generally in a good state of repair. The program of studies is predominantly academic, and college entrance requirements occupy a major portion of the time. Long thinks that the program of studies constitutes the most baffling and complex problem in Negro secondary education in North Carolina. The Division of Negro Education takes the point of view that curricular offerings should be the same for both Negro and white races. Others favor adaptation to the peculiar needs of a minority group. Long offers no solution, but recommends study of the problem in great detail. With reference to the aims and interests of students he finds that secondary students entertain vocational aims they will never attain. Failure of attainment is, in most cases, due to factors involving finances or mental ability. The lack of a program of guidance in public secondary schools for Negroes is bound to lead to much disappointment and maladjustment.

Florida[43] sponsored a state survey of its public schools, which very frankly sets forth the favorable and unfavorable aspects with respect to the education of Negroes. Conditions were reported as "spotty." Unsatisfactory conditions were caused, usually, by official neglect. Generally speaking, the State authorities were more friendly than local authorities. County Superintendents did not supervise their Negro schools. The curricula of Negro schools lacked adaptation to the needs of the group which the schools were intended to serve. Atten-

[43]*Educational Survey Commission and Survey Staff Report to the Legislature of the State of Florida.* Bureau of Publications, Teachers College, Columbia University, New York City, 1929.
Educational Survey Commission. *Official Report on The Education of Negroes in Florida.* Reprint by the State Department of Education, Tallahassee, Florida.

tion is called to the fact that the state supervision of Negro schools has been ineffective, and subsequent development of Negro high schools calls for intelligent guidance.

The County Training Schools, with one or two exceptions, were not doing the work for which they were intended, nor were they contributing what they might contribute to the progress of Negro education.[44]

Any other Southern state would find in this report an example for self criticism concerning the status of its provision for the education of its Negroes. The survey could have been more effectively presented if significant data for elementary and secondary levels had been clearly distinguished.

W. E. Turner[45] treats the development of secondary schools for Negroes in Tennessee. As early as 1899 there was established in Nashville a school offering high school work, but according to Turner the work amounted to little more than seventh grade work. It is interestingly pointed out that in 1915, when S. L. Smith attempted to establish County Training Schools in three densely Negro populated counties—Haywood, Shelby and Fayette—he found it impossible to find students prepared for high school work. The first high school in Tennessee to be approved by the State Department of Education, or any other accrediting agency, was the County Training School at Dyersburg. It was approved in 1920.

The history and status of Negro education in East Texas has been traced by W. R. Davis.[46] Little progress in secondary education was made before 1911, when the law for classification of high schools was passed, calling for grouping by the State Department of Education into schools of first, second, and third class. The major development in Negro secondary schools came in the last decade, for prior to 1925 little attempt was made by the State to classify Negro schools. In 1931 only 47 out of 300 schools had been classified by the committee on classification.

[44]Educational Survey Commission. *Official Report on the Education of Negroes in Florida*, p. 23.
[45]Turner, W. E. *A Survey of Negro High Schools in Tennessee*. Unpublished Masters' Thesis, University of Tennessee, Knoxville, Tenn., 1932.
[46]Davis, W. R. *The Development and Present Status of Negro Education in East Texas*. Bureau of Publications, Teachers College, Columbia University, New York, N. Y., 1934.

Davis found that insufficient laboratory equipment and library facilities, excessive size of classes, short terms, low salaries, and inadequate buildings retarded the growth of classified Negro secondary schools. While Negroes constitute one-third of the total scholastic population of Texas, only 47 classified high schools have been developed, as contrasted with 848 such high schools for white students. He believes that the County Training School movement promises to relieve the Negro secondary problem, as it is an attempt to supply the need for consolidated rural high schools.

Summary

These studies considered as a whole indicate that great progress has been made in the development of secondary education for Negroes during the past 18 years. The development, however, has not been uniform and great variation characterizes the secondary educational facilities provided by the several states or by the counties of a single state.

An accurate account of the actual status of public Negro secondary education in the Southern states cannot be obtained from these studies.

Differences in secondary school facilities provided for the two races are stressed in these studies and in most cases are in favor of the majority group. It is quite evident that there is still much to be done in providing for the education of Negroes if they are to be granted an opportunity to utilize education for what it is worth.

Chapter II

THE DEVELOPMENT OF COUNTY TRAINING SCHOOLS IN THE SOUTH

SOUTH of that somewhat vague boundary known as the Mason-Dixon line, public education has, for many years, been facing the social, political and economic problems involved in seeking ways and means whereby two races might live together under difficult conditions. While the task of providing educational facilities for the majority race was difficult, it was more so with reference to the Negro. The persistent and deep-rooted misunderstandings and prejudices about interracial relations forced the South, with its low per capita wealth,[1] to support two systems of schools. Under the handicap of interracial differences, poverty and ignorance, progress in Negro education has, in most respects, lagged decidedly behind education for whites. Those persons concerned with the progress of Negro education have been faced, not only with the problem of stimulating better educational provisions, but also with the necessity of adapting education to the prevailing aspects of Negro rural life in the South. The County Training Schools resulted from the attempt to meet this need.

THE BEGINNING OF THE COUNTY TRAINING SCHOOL MOVEMENT

Throughout the Southern states which maintain separate schools for the two races, mention of County Training Schools for Negroes usually leads to a consideration of the John F. Slater Fund.[2]

In the year 1882, Mr. John F. Slater, of Norwich, Connecticut, founded the Fund which bears his name. The committal

---

[1] Average per capita wealth of the South was $1,785; the non-South $3,609 and the United States $3,088 in 1929-1930. See McCuistion, Fred. *Financing Schools in the South, 1930.* (Issued by State Directors of Educational Research as a part of the Proceedings of the Conference held at Peabody College, December 5th and 6th, 1930, Cotton States Building, Nashville, Tennessee, p. 30.) p. 6.

[2] For purposes of this study, only schools assisted by the Slater Fund as County Training Schools are considered. The states maintaining separate schools for the races follow: Alabama, Arkansas, Delaware, Florida, Georgia, Kentucky, Louisiana, Maryland, Mississippi, Missouri, North Carolina, Oklahoma, South Carolina, Tennessee, Texas, Virginia and West Virginia.

Development of County Training Schools in South 25

letter which was written to the first Board of Trustees on March 4, 1882, stated that he was motivated in the establishment of such a fund by the precedent set by the Peabody Education Fund.[3] The sum of $1,000,000 was appropriated for the establishment of the Slater Fund for the general purpose of uplifting the lately emancipated population of the Southern states and their posterity by conferring on them the blessings of a Christian education.[4] The "largest liberty" as to changing methods of applying the income of the fund was given, and authority was granted to invest the capital, after a lapse of thirty years, in order to make advantages for education more accessible to poor students of the Negro race. The fund was to be administered in no partisan, sectional, or sectarian spirit. The Honorable Rutherford B. Hayes was designated as the first president of the corporation. This Educational Fund was the first ever to devote its entire efforts toward improvement of Negro educational opportunities. At the fourth meeting of the Trustees held on October 16, 1883, a matter of policy was stated as follows:

"RESOLVED, that . . . in all cases where appropriations are made to schools, colleges, or institutions . . . it is particularly desirable to make such appropriations dependent upon a like or larger sum being raised for the same specific purpose by the parties interested."[5]

It is significant that nearly all other educational foundations have been substantially in agreement with this policy. On February 6, 1883, Congress passed a joint resolution expressing appreciation for Mr. Slater's philanthropy and appropriated the money necessary to provide a gold medal, which was later presented to him.

It has been said that the first great educational fund was the Peabody Education Fund, and The John F. Slater Fund was the second.[6]

While County Training Schools have been supported co-

---

[3] Trustees of the John F. Slater Fund. *Documents Relating to the Origin and Work of the Slater Trustees.* Occasional Papers, No. 1, 1894, pp. 9-10.
[4] *Ibid.*, p. 10.
[5] The John F. Slater Fund. *Proceedings and Reports,* For Year Ending June 30, 1932, p. 2.
[6] Ayers, Leonard P. *Seven Great Foundations.* Department of Child Hygiene, Russell Sage Foundation, New York, 1911, pp. 23-27.

operatively at various times by at least seven different sources,[7] credit for the early stimulation of this development is allocated to the John F. Slater Fund by common acknowledgment of competent authorities.[8]

The facts which led to the establishment of one of the first of these schools tell a story of wider significance than the specific school situation itself.

On April 9, 1910, Professor A. M. Strange, B.S., the Negro principal of the Graded School in Collins, Mississippi, wrote to Dr. James H. Dillard, the general agent of the Slater Fund and President of the Anna T. Jeanes Foundation, for assistance in the employment of an industrial teacher for the girls. "The aim of the school is to specialize two lines of work, viz: Scientific Agriculture for the boys and the domestic sciences for the girls. Hence the import of this letter to you is asking aid in the interest of the girls."

By September of the same year, Strange had left Collins, Mississippi, for he wrote next from Kentwood, Louisiana. This time he was soliciting aid for a school to be known as the "Kentwood A. and I. Institute." Evidently Dr. Dillard was interested in the idea, for on November 17, 1910, Strange wrote a letter, part of which will be quoted. It eloquently reveals the growing economic problems of the races and the cooperative means through which the early movement for public secondary schools for Negroes gained impetus. Part of the original letter in uncorrected form is quoted below:

---

[7] The Federal Government through Smith-Hughes aid, State tax funds, county and local tax funds, the General Educational Board, the Carnegie Corporation, the Rosenwald Fund and the John F. Slater Fund.

[8] Brawley, Benjamin. *Doctor Dillard of the Jeanes Fund.* Fleming H. Revell Company, New York City, 1930, pp. 74-76.

Caldwell, B. C. "The Work of the Jeanes and Slater Funds," *Annals of American Academy of Political and Social Sciences,* No. 36, pp. 172-177.

Caliver, Ambrose. *Secondary Education for Negroes,* p. 33.

Dillard, James Hardy. "School Help in the Open Country," *Opportunity,* Vol. 1, No. 3, 1923, pp. 10-12.

Dillard, James Hardy. "A Happy Development," *Opportunity,* Vol. 8, January, 1930, pp. 14-16.

Jones Lance, G. E. *Negro Schools in the Southern States,* pp. 111-117.

Jones, Thomas Jesse. *Negro Education: A Study of Private and Higher Schools for Colored People in the United States,* pp. 37-38.

Jones, Thomas Jesse. *Twenty Year Report of the Phelps-Stokes Fund, 1911-1931.* The Phelps-Stokes Fund, New York City, 1932, pp. 46, 53.

Leavell, Ullin W. *Philanthropy in Negro Education,* pp. 95; 119.

Development of County Training Schools in South

"... I note from the tone of your letter that you are deeply interested in our welfare. These is but one hope for the Negro, as a mass in the Southland, and that hope is to have him imbibe and inculcate the idea of going back to the farm and there make good. We see daily, facts demonstrated concerning the negro in the trades. Since the northern white mechanics have come into the southland with their unionized system of labor, painting, carpentry, brickmasonary and various other bread winning persuits which go to make up a working man's support in the city are now being closed to the negro, it is only a question of time when the negro as an entiety will be counted out of the trade life of the city. With above stated facts we naturally conclude that the best form of education for the mass of negroes in Southland is that form which will send him with head, heart and hand trained, back to farm buy small plats of land build good homes cultivate their 10 or 12 acres persue the tenor of their way and make substantial progress.

"We have succeeded in interesting the good white people of this section of parish and parish board of education to help us put the before mentioned idea into execution. This school fosters the idea of having boys learn scientific agriculture, dairying and horticulture for girls sewing, domestic economy, cooking, dairying and poultry raising. We have cleaned up 10 acres and will soon begin fencing. We need at least $4000.00 to finish our building and get in running order. We therefore ask you as a conservative southern gentleman, to help us in this movement, the best and conservative white ladies and gentlemen of this section are doing everything to make movement succeed. The mills have donated lumber, brickyard brick, the negro laborers at the mills have signed petition to give 25c monthly for support of institution .... We believe if this school succeeds with this unique idea of education it's promoters must be southern men who know every phase of negro life. We have 1500 acres of land reserved for colored people cut up in 5 acre lots for trucking to put the school's idea into execution.

"Thanking you for your kind letter and hoping that you will become further interested in our work as one of it's promoters."
"Make donation to the Kentwood A. and I. Institute.
Respectfully yours,
A. M. STRANGE."

Dr. Dillard's reply of November 23, 1910, is interesting and important. He reminded Strange that there had been numerous attempts to establish private colored industrial institutes throughout the South, attempts which had met with varying degrees of success. Further along he states:

"What I am greatly desirous of seeing is that . . . attempts should be directed in the line of simply establishing a high school for the county or parish, which may some day be part of the public school system. I wish, therefore, that the name of your institution were Agricultural and Industrial High School, because the word high school carries with it the local idea, which I think is the proper one."

At a time when secondary education of Negroes was almost entirely dependent on private institutions, and when most of the public secondary schools then existing for Negroes were in large cities,[9] this attitude of Dr. Dillard's was significant. In brief, it indicates a recognition of the importance of enlisting public support in the development of Negro secondary education and, at the same time, would encourage making these schools available to the majority of Negroes, since they reside in rural areas.

Evidence that Dr. Dillard's ideas were favorably received is seen in the reproduction on the next page of the letter of December 2, 1910, and the hand-bill sent to the Slater Fund office early the following year. The school was to be a high school, the property was deeded to the parish board of education, and A. C. Lewis, the local Superintendent of Education, approved the project.

The scholastic year 1911-1912 marks the beginning of the County Training School Movement as far as the Slater Fund is concerned. Superintendent Lewis of Tangipahoa Parish, working with Dr. Dillard, B. C. Caldwell, the Field Agent of the Slater Fund, and Strange, worked out plans whereby the "Kentwood A. & I. High School"[10] was changed to the "Tangipahoa Parish Training School for Colored Children." The school board agreed to furnish teachers and equipment, and the Slater Fund gave assistance to the amount of $500 toward the salary of an industrial teacher in the school. Lewis recognized in this type of rural secondary school a potential means of improving the preparation of rural teachers. This, then, is the account of the establishment of the first of these schools. At the same time it is probably the account of the beginning of one of the first public rural secondary schools for Negroes in the United States.

Requisitions for Slater Fund aid which came from three

---

[9] Jones, Thomas Jesse. *Negro Education: A Study of Private and Higher Schools for Colored People in the United States*, pp. 41-43.

[10] "A. & I." stood for "Agricultural and Industrial" in this case. A. C. Lewis is now a State Agent for Negro Education in Louisiana.

TRUSTEES:
Dr. J. H. Ellis, President.
W. K. Amacker Sec. & Treas. (Cashier Kentwood Bank)
J. W. Morgan.
W. D. Welsh, Mayor.
S. H. McLaughlin, (Gen. Salesman Brooks-Scanlon Lumber Co.)
J. S. Foley, (Gen. Mgr. Brooks-Scanlon Lumber Co.)

12/7

Kentwood A. & I. High School.
A. M. Strange, Principal.

Kentwood, La., Dec., 2, 1910.

Dr. Jas. H. Dillard,
New Orleans, La.

Dear Sir:

Your kind and most considerate letter came to hand a few days ago and it was a great source of delight to us to know that you were interested in us. We thank you very kindly for the timely and appropriate suggestion of changing the name from institute to high school which, as you say, carries the local idea. It is our aim to have this school become a part of the public school system of this parish, from the fact that we have deeded our property to the parish board of education.

We would consider it quite a treat should you or the field agent come to see what we are doing. Mr. W.K. Amacker, one of the trustees of this school, who was one of the students of Tulane University when you were Dean, told me to mehtion the fact that it would be a treat to us to have YOU come and look the affair over with us.

Hoping you can arrange affairs so that you can get up and see us ere long and become a life long friend to this institution.

Looking for a favorably reply soon, we beg to remain

Yours Respectfully

A. M. Strange

x This is something of the idea I had with reference to work the state fund might form — A.H.D.

REPRODUCTION OF A LETTER PERTAINING TO THE BEGINNING OF THE COUNTY TRAINING SCHOOL MOVEMENT FOR NEGROES IN THE SOUTH.

(*Notice Dr. James Hardy Dillard's Note on the Margin of the Letter.*)

Kentwood A. & I. High School.
A. M. Strange, Principal.

Kentwood, La.,

To

    This introduces to you A. M. Strange, principal of the Kentwood, Agricultural and Industrial High School for colored, located at Kentwood, La. Of all the negro educators in the United States, we believe that his idea is the only correct one. He believes that his people are peculiarly adapted to "till the soil" and that tilling the soil is their place as a mass, in American Civilization.

    He believes that on account of the number of white mechanics coming from the north, with their superior skill and their unionized system of labor the negro mechanic will soon be relegated to the rear and that bread winning persuit will soon be closed to him. Being unprepared to meet these conditions and in a state of hand-to-mouth existence he will soon become a burden on public charity and a nuisance to progress.

    He believes that worthy negroes who wish to build homes and be a part of this country's future greatness should be encouraged to go back to the farm and there make good. He believes that the men and companies that own large tracts of land could do the negro the greatest favor of their lives by cutting those tracts of land up into 5 and 10 acre plots and offering inducements to go on that land, build homes, become producers and economical consumers, thereby adding to the wealth and comfort of Dixie.

    He believes when the South gets ready to inoculate the negro into it's civic life it will do so and not before and all the agitation under the sun along this line is of no good. Prof. Strange is trying to put these ideas into execution through the school that he is fostering. He enjoys the absolute confidence of the conservative and best white people of this section. The school needs money to put these ideas into execution; therefore we the undersigned members of the board of trustees of above mentioned Institution beg of you to give him a chance to meet your city at large and address an audience in some public hall and then the various Commercial agencies whose motto is: "For a Greater Louisiana," and subscribe liberally to this movement. We feel that the movement is worthy of public notice, hence we appeal to you and city to help same.

    Kindly notify A. M. Strange when he can have the opportunity of meeting your people.

J. H. ELLIS, Pres.	S. H. MCLAUGHLIN,
A. K. AMACKER, Sect.-Treas.	W. D. WELSH,
J. W. MORGAN,	S. FOLEY,
A. C. LEWIS, Supt. of Education.	A. B. LEE, Pres. Police Jury.

REPRODUCTION OF PRINTED FORM USED BY A. M. STRANGE WHO HELPED TO ESTABLISH THE FIRST PARISH TRAINING SCHOOL IN LOUISIANA.

other county superintendents in 1911 indicated that the need was felt for one larger and better school in each county.[11] It, also, was recognized that trained teachers could not be had for the meager salaries paid rural Negro teachers in the primitive elementary schools. Through this superior county school, each of these superintendents hoped to get a regular and fairly good supply of teachers trained to do the work needed in their respective counties. On February 3, 1911, Dr. Dillard, when replying to a request for aid from J. H. Cole, principal of a Negro school in Newton, Mississippi, stated:

"If there be any disposition on the part of the school authorities to start a sort of industrial high school in the county, I should be glad to cooperate, but I would want to know from Superintendent Mabry something definite about the proposition."

The school was built, subsequently, through the cooperative efforts of the Newton County public school officials, the town of Newton, an organization of colored people who contributed, and a pledge of $500 a year for three years on the part of the Slater Fund.

Largely through the efforts of Superintendent M. A. Madlock, of Hope, Arkansas, and H. C. Yerger, the principal of the Negro school known as the Shover School, in Hope, the Hempstead County Training School was established. In this case, the Shover School was converted into the central training school for Hempstead County. This was accomplished through funds from the state and town school authorities, subscriptions from the local cotton-business men, individual contributions of white and Negro citizens, and the Slater appropriation. A statement made on March 9, 1934, by H. C. Yerger, who is still the principal of the school he helped to establish in 1911, follows:

". . . It originated during the administration of Professor M. A. Madlock, who was City Superintendent at that time. Mr. Madlock received a letter from Dr. Dillard asking him to suggest what best use could be made of a small sum of money which he had for this school. Mr. Madlock gave me the letter to answer and I suggested that support be given to a centrally located school where colored rural school teachers could attend after their teaching terms were out. At

---

[11]Favrot, Leo. *County Training Schools for Negroes in the South*, pp. 4; 10.

that time the majority of colored rural teachers in this section were below the High School level in their preparation . . . . It is my opinion that we would not have had High Schools for Negroes in Arkansas as early as we did if they had not been brought under the disguise of County Training Schools."

This excerpt from the minutes of the Hope School Board indicates that the public school authorities were responsive to the offer:

"Be it resolved by the Hope School Board in special session assembled: That it pledge itself to construct and equip suitable buildings for an industrial department in connection with the Negro school of this district, provided an appropriation of $500.00 a year for three years shall be guaranteed by the trustess of the Slater Fund to employ a teacher for said department and to maintain the same.

"Resolved further that a copy of these resolutions be given T. B. Caldwell and a copy sent to James H. Dillard.

"Done by the Hope School Board in special session assembled this the 25th day of August, 1911.

J. D. COTTON, *President*."

In Sabine Parish, Louisiana, the Sabine Normal and Industrial Institute, a community school seven miles out in the country, was made the Parish Training School through the efforts of Superintendent W. S. Mitchell and R. E. Jacobs, principal of the school. Support came from the parish tax funds, liberal donations from the timber interests owning land surrounding the school, and the Slater Fund's $500 yearly contribution.

In the establishment of these first County Training Schools no one pattern was carried out. In each instance it was fundamentally a problem of local adaptation to be worked out through a variety of cooperative sources involving both races. There were, however, several common factors in each situation.

1. A recognized need for a bigger and better school to offer to Negroes in the county or parish a more advanced education than that afforded by the rural elementary schools.
2. The recognition of the need for better prepared teachers for the county or parish.
3. The frequent mention of agricultural and industrial education.
4. The willingness to cooperate in order to secure the support of a philanthropic organization.

Policies Effective in County Training School Establishment

It has been shown that as early as 1910, Dr. Dillard was committed to a policy of encouraging the establishment of public high schools for Negroes in county and parish systems of schools. The resources of the Slater Fund were directed toward financial cooperation with local agencies who were willing to share in initial expenditures and in continuing the support of such educational undertakings.

Certain requirements were attached to grants from the Slater Fund. These conditions were designed to strengthen the sense of responsibility of public authorities for providing more advanced educational facilities for Negroes in rural areas, and to raise the standards as rapidly as possible. At the same time these requirements helped to avoid the pauperizing tendencies which often characterize the mis-application of philanthropic effort. From the beginning, offers to assist in the establishment of County Training Schools have been made upon the basis of conditions in effect in 1911-12, which follow:

1. The school property shall belong to the state, county, or district, and the school shall be a part of the public school system.
2. There shall be an appropriation for salaries of not less than $750 from public funds raised by state, county, or district taxation.
3. The teaching shall extend through the eighth year with the intention of adding at least two years as soon as it shall be possible to make such extension.[12]

In the Proceedings and Reports for 1920, a further condition is indicated in that "the length of term shall be at least eight months."[13]

The Slater Fund made its appropriations to schools upon the understanding that aid would be discontinued after the schools had become well organized and the public school boards supported them completely. The following diminishing scale has been followed as closely as possible: $500 per year for the first three years, $250 annually for the next two years, and

---

[12] The John F. Slater Fund. *Proceedings and Reports*, For Year Ending September 30, 1919, pp. 11-13.
[13] The John F. Slater Fund. *Proceedings and Reports*, For Year Ending September 30, 1930, p. 12.

$100 for needed equipment after the expiration of the five years. It should be added, however, that this policy has not been pursued rigorously.

In 1923 the necessary appropriation for salaries from public funds was raised from $750 to $1,000[14] and in 1932 to $1,500, for certain localities.

In 1925 the requirement pertaining to "adding at least two years" was changed to "adding grades."[15] This was due probably to the fact that in 1924-25 there were forty County Training Schools which had reached the status of four-year high schools.

A recent modification which concerned Slater support for such schools for 1932-33 follows: ". . . Schools that have attained the status of four-year accredited state high schools be not considered as eligible for further aid from the funds of this Board."[16]

Another policy of significance concerns the disposition of the Slater Fund to encourage and facilitate cooperation of other foundations in developing the County Training Schools. The General Education Board has aided in the purchase of equipment and in building teachers' homes and dormitories. In 1920 it made an appropriation for teachers' salaries to be disbursed through the Slater Fund, to enable local school boards to raise the standard of the teaching force in these schools.[17] The conditions under which such aid could be secured stipulated that grants were to be decreased each year until after the lapse of five years, when the entire support of the teacher would be derived from local and state funds. This virtually tended to set a minimum salary schedule of $1,000 a year for principals, and $500 a year for teachers in new County Training Schools.

The Carnegie Corporation and The Peabody Fund have contributed sums, from time to time, to be distributed through the Slater Fund, for the purpose of increasing the number of

---

[14] The John F. Slater Fund. *Proceedings and Reports*, For Year Ending September 30, 1920, p. 12.

[15] The John F. Slater Fund. *Proceedings and Reports*, For Year Ending September, 1925, p. 10.

[16] Extract from the Minutes of the John F. Slater Board of Trustees in files of the Slater Fund office, 726 Jackson Place, N. W., Washington, D. C.

[17] Favrot, Leo. Op. cit., pp. 11-12.

County Training Schools in the several states.[18] Julius Rosenwald, as an individual and through the fund which bears his name, has aided, not only in the manner indicated above, but also by building many school houses and teachers' homes for County Training Schools, and by helping to supply standards for these buildings. When it is realized that these agencies have augmented the monies derived from Federal aid through the Smith-Hughes funds; the public support from local, county, and state tax funds; and the contributions of countless patrons of both races, this becomes a striking example of social cooperation in education.

In the graphic presentation shown in Figure 1, the cumulative effect of stimulation of public effort on behalf of these schools over twenty years is apparent. During this time the ratio of public monies paid for salaries in County Training Schools to sums disbursed through the Slater Fund for the same purpose grew from approximately one and a half to one in 1912, to almost eighteen to one in 1930. During the twenty year period the public expenditures for salaries in these schools were more than ten times the disbursement for this purpose through the Slater Fund. Evidently, the policy of stimulative assistance to promote effort and responsibility for public educational opportunities for Negroes was effective.

AIMS AND PURPOSES OF COUNTY TRAINING SCHOOLS

Since there were no precedents to follow in encouraging the development of these schools, the spread of the idea to other states and counties necessitated some determination of their aims and purposes to lend direction to the efforts of the schools already established and those to follow.

At a meeting of State Agents[19] and others interested in Negro education, a committee consisting of Messrs. Leo M. Favrot, James L. Sibley, and Jackson Davis was appointed to set forth the general aims and purposes of County Training Schools, and to formulate a suggested course of study for these

---

[18] The John F. Slater Fund. *Proceedings and Reports*, For Year Ending September 1930, p. 6.

[19] "State Agents" are agents for Negro education in the Southern States. They are appointed by the State Departments of Education and the General Education Board. The first one was appoined in 1910 by the Peabody Educational Fund and the Southern Educational Board. The next year the General Education Board took over the support of the Agents. By 1919, fifteen states had Agents.

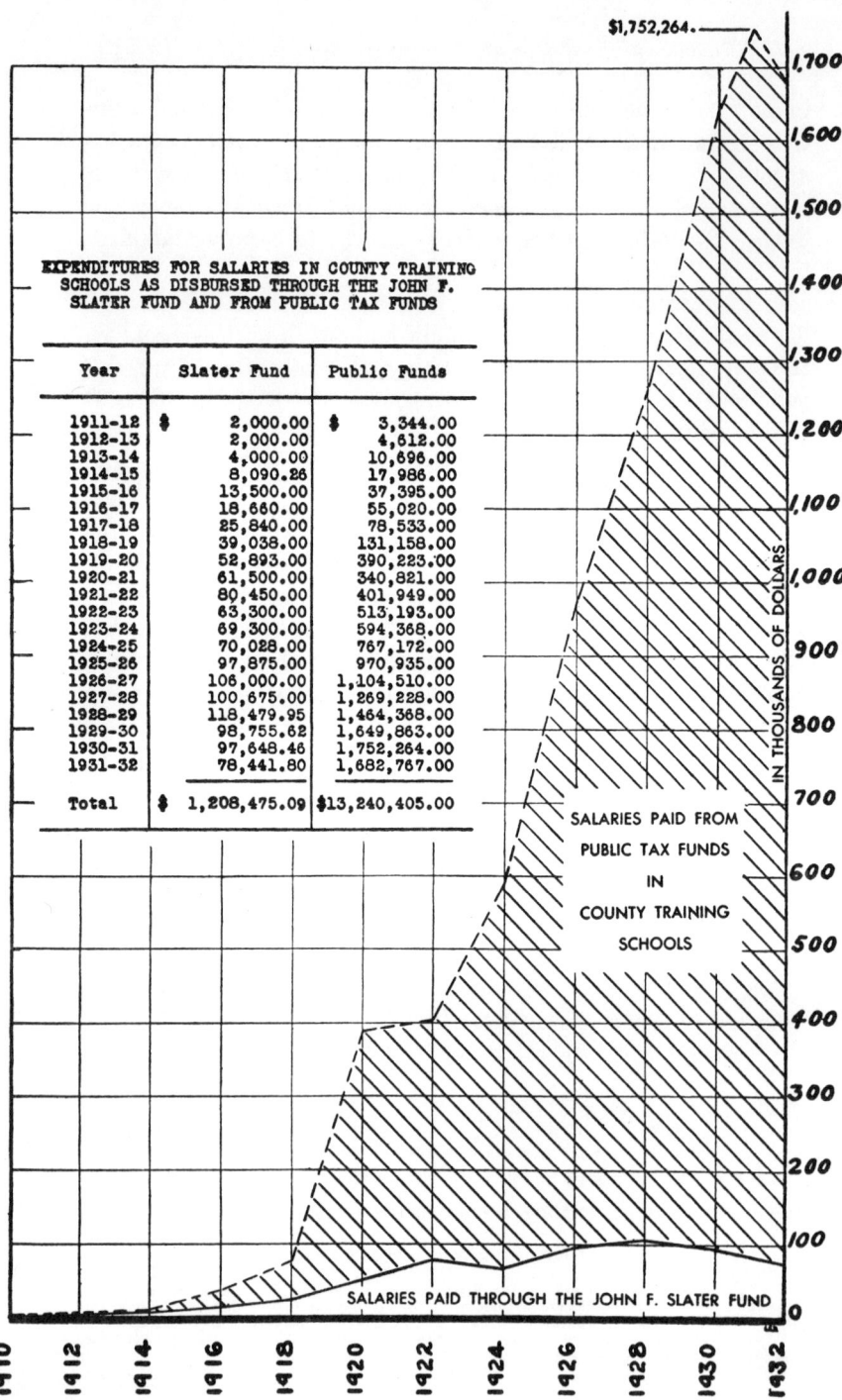

FIGURE 1. EXPENDITURES FOR SALARIES IN COUNTY TRAINING SCHOOLS AS DISBURSED THROUGH THE JOHN F. SLATER FUND AND FROM PUBLIC TAX FUNDS

schools. After several meetings wherein the opinions of county school boards, state departments of education, and the philanthropic groups assisting in the establishment and maintenance of these schools were considered, the following aims and purposes were presented:

1. "To supply for the county a central Negro public training school offering work two or three years in advance of that offered by the common schools.
2. "To establish a type of Negro school in the county which shall serve as a model with respect to physical plant and equipment, teaching force, course of study, and plan of operation.
3. "To lay emphasis on thorough work in all common school studies, to relate these studies to the lives of the pupils, and to develop standards of achievement.
4. "To give industrial training, laying particular emphasis upon subjects pertaining to home and farm.
5. "To prepare Negro boys and girls to make a good living and lead a useful life by knowing how to care for the home, to utilize land, to make home gardens, to raise their own meat, poultry products, milk products, etc.
6. "To prepare young men and young women to become rural and elementary school teachers, by enabling them to meet legal requirements of the state, by giving them a closer acquaintance and sympathy with rural activities, and by supplying such elementary professional training as will help them to secure the best results in this work. The need in the South for properly qualified Negro rural teachers is everywhere apparent."[20]

In short, the purpose of the County Training School was to offer a more advanced education, based upon a necessary adaptation to the demands of rural life and to the training of teachers for the rural schools within the county.

By 1924 it was evident that these Training Schools would ultimately become high schools.[21] In the beginning, however, these schools offered work that rarely extended through the eighth grade, and it would have been inaccurate to call them high schools. It seems that J. D. Eggleston, who was at one time State Superintendent of Public Instruction of Virginia, and who

---

[20] The Trustees of the John F. Slater Fund. *Suggested Course for County Training Schools.* Occasional Papers No. 18, 1917, pp. 11-12.
[21] The John F. Slater Fund. *Proceedings and Reports,* For Year Ending September 30, 1924, p. 12.

The John F. Slater Fund.

County Training Schools

One of the greatest immediate needs is for even fairly competent teachers in the small public schools. The Slater Fund has contributed much to the preparation of teachers, but in the past its contributions in this direction have been mainly to the larger and higher institutions. There is now great need for the preparation of teachers in a lower grade of advancement. The immediate conditions under which such work must be done may be far from ideal, but the effort faces facts as they are. It is a fact that a very large majority of the teachers in the small rural schools for Negroes have got what they have of education and training in their own or a neighboring county. Many superintendents are showing interest in the improvement of some central school in the county which may serve the purpose of supplying a somewhat better grade of teachers.

Such is the origin of the so-called County Training Schools of which we have aided in making a beginning. In 1912 there were three, in 1913 four, in 1914 eight, in 1915 seventeen. For the next session we propose to aid in about thirty, provided the reasonable conditions are fulfilled. These conditions, as previously approved, are:

First, that the school property shall belong to the State or county, thus fixing the school as a part of the public school system;

Second, that there shall be an appropriation of at least $750 from the public funds for maintenance;

Third, that the teaching shall be carried strictly and honestly through at least the eighth grade, including industrial work, and in the last year some training, however elementary, for the work of teaching.

Under these conditions the Slater Fund has agreed to appropriate $500 for maintenance, and in the first year, where new buildings or repairs may be necessary, to aid in supplying these in cooperation with amounts raised from other sources. (Extract from Report of Director, April 28, 1915.)

REPRODUCTION OF A BULLETIN SENT OUT BY DR. DILLARD PERTAINING TO THE ESTABLISHMENT OF COUNTY TRAINING SCHOOLS

later became President of Hampton-Sidney College and a member of the Slater Board, suggested that they be called *County Training Schools*, and that, when they had developed into high schools, they be so termed.[22] As the training school movement gained momentum, the aim to develop these schools into regular four-year high schools gained impetus.

Many schools formerly listed as County Training Schools have now become wholly supported by public funds and are listed as rural high schools. Certain private and denominational schools, by arrangement with county school officials, have become County Training Schools.[23] There would be no objection to calling these schools "high schools," but the term "County Training School" is traditional in many communities, and is looked upon with especial favor.

TEACHER-TRAINING IN COUNTY TRAINING SCHOOLS

At the time the training school movement had its inception relatively few Negro teachers in rural elementary schools had more than the crudest kind of elementary education. Even as late as 1930 more than 18,130 of the Negro teaching force in 15 Southern states had less than a high school education.[24] Mississippi, alone, had 1,312 Negro elementary teachers who had only an elementary school background.[25] From this it can be seen that County Training Schools, by merely offering secondary work, gave their graduates a formal education superior to that of the strictly rural elementary teacher. The teacher-training function of these schools, however, went further than this.

From the very beginning of the movement the authorities actively concerned with the actual establishment of the County Training Schools were entirely cognizant of the practical opportunities the schools offered for giving Negroes a simple preparation for teaching in the rural schools of the county

[22] The Slater Fund. *Proceedings and Reports*, For Year Ending September 30, 1929, p. 13.
[23] The Slater Fund. *Proceedings and Reports*, For Year Ending June 30, 1932, p. 17.
[24] McCuistion, Fred. *The South's Negro Teaching Force*. The Julius Rosenwald Fund, Nashville, Tennessee, 1931, p. 19.
[25] *A Teaching Training Program for Colored Schools in Mississippi*. Bulletin No. 61, September, 1930, State Department of Education, Jackson, Mississippi, pp. 13-15.

wherein the Training School was located. It should be mentioned that the responsible officials cooperating in the operation of a County Training School are the county school board members and the superintendent. In addition to these officials, the State Agents for Negro Education, besides assisting the field agents of the Slater Fund in selecting suitable locations, also serve as advisers and supervisors in planning the work of the schools and assisting in the selection of capable teachers. It was a group of these men who formulated a course of study for these schools in 1917.[26] Included in the printed version, copies of which were sent to all such schools, was the following course recommended for teacher-training:

1. *Observation and Practice Teaching*
   (60-minute period daily.) The first five grades are used as the practice school and the primary teacher is usually in charge of the teaching work.
2. *Elementary Principles of Teaching.*
   (30-minute period daily, one-half year.) The principles are to be worked into practice in teaching.
3. *School Management.*
   (30-minute period daily, one-half year.)

No organized program approaching a professional level, however, was attempted in the majority of these schools.

The exact extent of the teacher-training activities of these schools will never be known. In 1921 a study[27] of the subjects listed by principals in 107 County Training Schools indicated that "Principles of Teaching" and "Practice Teaching" were listed 20 times. "Methods" was mentioned in 17 instances and "School Management" appeared 15 times. Since the number of County Training Schools has grown steadily, it is likely that numerous other schools have offered, at one time or another, modest courses.

As teacher-training facilities at the college level developed, the opportunity for the public secondary school to discharge this function naturally diminished. With higher standards for certification paralleling this development in professional education for Negroes, the opportunities for graduates of teach-

[26] Davis, Jackson, Dillard, James Hardy, Favrot, Leo, Sibley, James L. and others. *A Suggested Course of Study for County Training Schools for Negroes in the South.* The John F. Slater Fund, Washington, D. C.
[27] Favrot, Leo. *op cit., pp.* 74-75.

er-training departments in public secondary schools to be placed diminished proportionately. In 1930 eight hundred-forty-one students were graduated from teacher-training departments of Negro secondary schools.[28] Of this number, 765 came from Alabama, Florida, Georgia and Louisiana. All of these states issued teaching certificates at that time, only to persons having completed work for graduation in a school doing work approved by the State. Just how many of these came from Training Schools cannot be ascertained. It is highly improbable that many came from Alabama.[29] It is probable that at that time the County Training Schools of Florida and Georgia carried on a relatively small amount of teacher training in an unofficial way. By 1932, however, except for Louisiana, all these states had very definitely abolished teacher-training work in the public Negro secondary schools.

Louisiana, almost from the beginning, has utilized these schools to serve two principal purposes. One is to provide secondary work for Negro youth, and the other "to train teachers for the rural schools."[30] In 1930 there were 28 public Parish Training Schools[31] wherein the teacher-training work was done in the tenth or eleventh grade.[32] This work, today, is directly in charge of an experienced teacher, termed the "teacher trainer." Each school is carefully supervised by members of the Division of Negro Education in the State Department of Education. State teachers' certificates are issued to graduates who have reached eighteen years of age.

With the exception of Louisiana and a few schools scattered throughout several states, the teacher-training function discharged by County Training Schools is no longer of primary importance.

GROWTH OF THE COUNTY TRAINING SCHOOL MOVEMENT

By March, 1913, Dr. Dillard was convinced of the value of these "county industrial training schools,"[33] and wrote to

[28] McCuistion, Fred. *Op. cit.*, p. 14.
[29] See quotation on page 93.
[30] Newbold, N. C. (Chairman.) *Report of the Committee of Investigation of Certain Phases of Negro Education in Louisiana.* State Department of Education, Baton Rouge, Louisiana, 1930. Section A, Part III, p. 10.
[31] Same as County Training Schools in other States.
[32] Louisiana has the 7-4 type of organization.
[33] The Trustees of the John F. Slater Fund. *County Teacher Training Schools for Negroes.* Occasional Papers, No. 14, 1913, p. 3.

TABLE II

DISTRIBUTION OF COUNTY TRAINING SCHOOLS IN FIFTEEN SOUTHERN STATES AS AIDED BY THE JOHN F. SLATER FUND EACH YEAR FROM 1911 TO 1932, INCLUSIVE

STATE	1911	1912	1913	1914	1915	1916	1917	1918	1919	1920	1921	1922	1923	1924	1925	1926	1927	1928	1929	1930	1931	1932	Number of Years Slater Fund Aided Schools in State
Alabama	1	..	1	1	4	6	7	11	14	14	15	17	20	24	29	33	35	37	38	35	34	29	20
Arkansas	1	1	1	2	4	4	5	5	6	7	9	10	12	14	15	16	20	23	25	24	26	21	22
Florida	..	..	..	..	..	..	..	1	1	1	..	2	4	5	6	9	10	15	18	12	9	10	14
Georgia	1	..	1	2	2	3	4	5	9	11	11	13	17	19	22	26	33	34	34	38	43	38	20
Kentucky	..	2	..	1	1	2	3	2	4	8	9	10	13	15	17	19	18	18	17	20	17	19	19
Louisiana	2	2	2	2	2	2	2	4	7	10	11	13	16	16	21	23	26	27	28	30	33	28	22
Maryland	..	..	..	..	..	..	..	1	2	2	2	2	2	2	2	2	2	2	..	..	..	..	11
Mississippi	1	1	2	1	..	2	3	4	4	11	13	16	21	23	27	29	29	33	33	34	35	36	21
Missouri	..	..	..	..	..	..	..	..	..	..	..	..	..	..	..	..	..	..	..	1	1	2	3
Oklahoma	..	..	..	..	..	..	..	..	..	1	3	5	5	5	7	6	7	7	7	7	8	5	13
Tennessee	..	..	..	3	3	4	5	6	9	11	13	14	15	17	18	19	22	22	22	24	26	26	18
N. Carolina	..	..	..	1	6	8	10	14	19	21	20	25	24	27	30	34	35	43	43	36	34	24	19
S. Carolina	..	..	..	1	1	3	4	6	9	12	13	15	17	21	29	33	35	37	38	40	39	34	19
Texas	..	..	..	1	2	2	4	5	7	10	13	13	13	14	19	22	24	27	29	31	33	34	19
Virginia	..	..	1	3	4	6	6	8	16	23	23	23	25	31	33	35	39	44	49	54	52	43	20
Total	4	4	8	17	29	42	53	72	107	142	155	178	204	233	275	306	335	369	381	386	390	349	

Development of County Training Schools in South 41

State Superintendents explaining the plan. He suggested that in many counties there were already central schools which might be turned, with small expense, into the type of school outlined. "The Slater Board is desirous of aiding more immediately than hitherto the educational conditions in rural districts and would be willing to cooperate with county boards and superintendents . . . ."[34]

Six State Superintendents of Education[35] expressed interest in the idea and promised cooperation. Table II[36] indicates that by 1915 all states with the exception of Florida, Maryland, Missouri and Oklahoma had one or more County Training Schools receiving assistance from the Slater Fund. The four states considered as exceptions have fewer Negro inhabitants in comparison with the other states listed. During the twenty-year period from 1911 to 1931 the number of County Training Schools assisted during a given year has grown from 4 to 390. The rapid increase probably indicates that the South recognized the value of the training schools; a conclusion which is substantiated by the great gain in support from public funds, which is shown in Figure 1, page 34.

Public support of County Training Schools was stimulated with marked success from 1920 to 1930. From 1911 to 1920 the annual number of schools assisted increased from 4 to 142, showing a gain of 138. From 1920 to 1930 the increase was 244. During the same interval, public support increased more than 300 per cent as compared with an increase of less than 100 per cent in the contributions disbursed through the Slater Fund.[37]

The number of County Training Schools assisted during a given year, the number of teachers, and the number of secondary school pupils enrolled annually shows a determined growth, and is indicated in Table III.

[34] *Ibid.*, p. 3.
[35] Henry J. Willingham, State Superintendent of Education of Alabama; W. M. Sheats, State Superintendent of Education of Florida; J. Y. Joyner, State Superintendent of Education of North Carolina; J. R. Brister, State Superintendent of Education of Tennessee; F. M. Barlley, State Superintendent of Education of Texas; and R. C. Stearnes, State Superintendent of Education of Virginia.
[36] Compiled by the author from data secured from the files of the John F. Slater Fund in Washington, D. C.
[37] Figure 1, page 34.

TABLE III
NUMBER OF COUNTY TRAINING SCHOOLS, TEACHERS, AND SECONDARY ENROLLMENT IN COUNTY TRAINING SCHOOLS, 1912 TO 1930[38]

Year	Number of Schools	Number of Teachers	SECONDARY ENROLLMENT Total	Average Number Per School
1911-12	4	20	77	19
1913-14	8	41	184	23
1915-16	29	135	404	14
1917-18	53	308	948	18
1919-20	107	624	1649	15
1921-22	155	963	3782	24
1923-24	204	1297	6189	30
1925-26	275	1889	9483	34
1927-28	335	2379	14092	42
1929-30	381	*	*	

* Data not available.

During the early years the average number of secondary pupils per school fluctuated owing to the fact that many of the schools aided as County Training Schools had to develop students to qualify for the upper grades. The steady growth of the secondary enrollment from 1920 on might have been due to several causes. In the first place it is quite possible that after ten years of activity, the County Training Schools were starting to develop the higher grades of secondary work. Then, too, the Julius Rosenwald Fund during the years from 1912 to 1920 assisted in the construction of 400 rural schoolhouses for Negro children.[39] By imposing conditions designed to stimulate, this Fund spurred support from local Negroes, whites, and public tax resources. Add to this the steady influence of the Jeanes Supervising Teachers whom the public increasingly has supported since 1912-13, and the cumulative effect of this growing cooperation in behalf of the Negro rural dweller is apparent.

Not only was there pronounced growth in the number of schools, but as Table IV indicates, the larger rural schools tended to develop into secondary schools.

[38]Compiled from the John F. Slater Fund *Proceedings and Reports*, and data in the files at the office of the Fund in Washington, D. C.
[39]Leavell, Ullin W. *Philanthrophy in Negro Education*, p. 118.

Development of County Training Schools in South   43

NUMBER OF TEACHERS AND ENROLLMENT, AND TEACHERS' SALARIES IN 23 COUNTY TRAINING SCHOOLS IN 10 SOUTHERN STATES. FOR 1917-18 AND 1932-33*

County, State	Number of Teachers 1918	Number of Teachers 1933	Enrollment Total 1918	Enrollment Total 1933	Above Grade 7 1918	Above Grade 7 1933	Teachers' Salaries Total 1918	Teachers' Salaries Total 1933	Average Annual Salary per Teacher 1918	Average Annual Salary per Teacher 1933
Picken, Alabama	4	6	105	182	11	71	$1,260	$3,940	$315	$657
Russell, Alabama	4	5	105	358	0	45	1,367	2,117	342	423
Dallas, Arkansas	8	10	416	554	56	104	2,640	3,840	330	384
Lee, Arkansas	8	9	625	481	17	116	3,960	3,906	495	434
Ben Hill, Georgia	5	8	224	584	9	37	1,320	3,285	264	411
Tift, Georgia	7	9	298	346	0	43	1,607	3,600	230	400
Morehouse, Louisiana	5	13	340	606	35	85	1,500	7,200	300	554
Covington, Mississippi	4	4	166	151	15	31	1,300	1,864	325	466
Lamar, Mississippi	4	7	148	295	23	38	1,303	1,890	326	270
Lee, Mississippi	7	16	285	766	31	202	2,210	8,595	316	557
Johnston, North Carolina	8	13	357	638	21	53	2,030	7,568	254	582
Pitt, North Carolina	5	7	149	203	1	39	1,525	4,432	305	633
Wake, North Carolina	5	11	161	512	12	104	2,225	6,596	445	600
Clarendon, South Carolina	6	9	320	417	30	68	1,830	4,800	305	533
Horry, South Carolina	5	11	260	453	5	57	1,440	5,800	288	527
Marion, South Carolina	8	16	412	738	19	125	3,120	7,290	390	456
Haywood, Tennessee	9	15	612	599	32	129	2,745	8,294	305	553
Madison, Tennessee	4	6	290	208	10	40	1,320	2,115	330	353
Guadalupe, Texas	6	6	126	220	13	76	2,591	3,800	432	633
Lavaca, Texas	3	5	113	80	15	32	1,616	1,880	539	376
Albemarle, Virginia	4	6	98	153	9	49	1,300	3,659	325	610
Greenville, Virginia	7	11	359	554	0	88	2,510	5,173	359	470
York, Virginia	5	8	127	206	9	55	1,600	6,800	320	850
TOTAL	131	211	6,096	9,304	373	1,687	$44,319	$108,444		
Per Cent Gain of 1932-33 over 1917-18	61%		52.6%		352.2%		144.7%			

*The data shown in this table for 1918 were taken from the study by Leo Favrot, *County Training School for Negroes, Occasional Papers No. 23*, The John F. Slater Fund, Charlottesville, Va., 1923, pp. 66-68. The figures for 1933 were taken from contracts between county superintendents and the Slater Fund; they are on file in the office of the Slater Fund in Washington, D. C.

Comparable data were available for 23 schools aided during the years between 1918 and 1933. During this time the total enrollment of these schools showed a gain of 52.6 per cent. At the same time the gain in enrollment above grade 7 jumped 352.2 per cent.[40] While five of these schools lost 287 from their total enrollment, they gained 259 in the higher grades. In 1918 the average enrollment above grade 7 was 16 pupils per school; in 1933 it was 73, in the same schools. The evidence points to the conclusion that these schools have shown a decided tendency to develop along secondary lines.

Another early objective of the Slater Fund was to improve the quality of instruction by defraying, in part, the salaries of teachers. During the fifteen-year interval the number of teachers employed increased 61 per cent. At the same time a gain of 144.7 per cent in expenditures for teachers' salaries occurred. In all except three cases the average annual salary per teacher showed gains ranging from 13 to 165 per cent. The data on salaries show an emphatic upward trend. If the widely held conception that better qualified teachers command higher salaries is true, then an improvement in instruction should have resulted in these schools.

The schools included in Table IV have been assisted by the Slater Fund for a longer period than is usual and consequently any conclusions pertaining to these schools must be considered somewhat empirically.

Perhaps the principle of diminishing returns operates in some cases involving philanthropic assistance. The case of the Lavaca County Training School in Texas is to the point, as is shown in Table IV. In 1918, each of three teachers received an average annual salary of $539, and they taught a total of 113 children, 15 of whom were in grades above the seventh. In 1933, each of five instructors in the same school received an average annual salary of $376, and they instructed 80 children, 32 of whom were in grade seven or above. In almost identical fashion, comparisons could be made for the Training Schools in Covington and Lamar counties in Mississippi. In the cases cited above the growth of the schools does not compare favor-

---

[40] Georgia, Louisiana, North Carolina, South Carolina, Texas and Virginia have 7-4 grade organizations.

ably with others included in Table IV. With 410 counties possessing a considerable Negro secondary population practically without any public high school facilities, it would be justifiable to withdraw aid from schools in this category and apply the philanthropic assistance elsewhere. This should not be done, however, until a careful study of each school has been made.

CHARACTERISTICS OF COUNTY TRAINING SCHOOLS

The large majority of County Training Schools were, in their early days, somewhat larger elementary schools located in rural areas wherein the Negro population tended to be dense. Frequently the smaller neighboring elementary schools were absorbed into these larger and more centrally located schools. While certain of them offered some secondary work at the time they were selected to serve as Training Schools, most of them had to evolve gradually into high school status. As the demand for more advanced education increased and means for providing it were made available, the secondary grades were added. Today in many counties in the South this same developmental cycle is in process in County Training Schools. In practically every case the enrollment is largely centered in the elementary grades. The sizes of these schools vary tremendously, ranging from slightly more than 100 pupils to well over 800. The average Training School in 1933 possessed a student body numbering 300 students, of which 46 were to be found in the secondary grades. From this general account it can be seen that these schools represent a somewhat unusual type of consolidated school development.

Some of the schools which are located in the larger urban communities have tended to develop along conventional American high school lines. On the other hand, the large majority, which are located in the open country or in small rural places, tend to adapt their educational offerings to the needs of the rural constituencies they are intended to serve. The attempt to aid the rural Negro is reflected in many ways. Practically all Training Schools offer instructional and laboratory facilities in the agricultural, industrial, and domestic sciences. These services are usually made available to both students and adults residing in the county. Invariably the "Smith-Hughes-teacher" is placed in these schools, and not infrequently he serves as the principal of the school. In attempting to make these schools more available to students from distant parts of the county, dormitories are at times included as part of the physical plant. In 1927 there were 66 Training schools possessing dormitory facilities for students.[41] The problem of providing suitable living accommodations for teachers is nowhere more serious than in connection with Negro rural schools. Teachers' homes were included as part of the plant in 98 schools in 1927.[42] Because so many of these schools are the largest or the only secondary schools in the counties wherein they are located, much of the community, social and general activity of the Negro population centers in them. Efforts to harmonize the interests of County Training Schools and the communities which they serve have in many cases met with marked success.

A better conception of the general nature of these schools can be gained from a description of several of them. While the following examples naturally are not typical of all of these schools, they give a general impression of the physical set-up, and show what is being done in some of them. The data presented below are taken from records which were made by the author while visiting schools on a field trip.

Warren County Training School, Wise, North Carolina.

This county is inhabited by 23,000 persons, of whom 15,000 are Negroes. Two schools offer secondary work—the County Training School and the J. R. Hawkins High School at Warrenton. Each school serves, roughly, half of the county. Largely through the financial efforts of the Negroes themselves and the Rosenwald Fund, fifteen buses have been secured. With the exception of a small section of the county possessing only paths for roads, every section can offer the Negro youth an opportunity for high school educational facilities at public expense. This county serves as an excellent example of what can be done in providing transportation.

The County Training School is located in the open country. The physical plant consists of an eleven-room brick building erected in 1931 to replace a frame structure destroyed by a tornado; one four-room frame structure housing the seventh grade and the elementary school library; another frame building wherein the agricultural, industrial, and domestic science classes are conducted; a combination

---

[41]The John F. Slater Fund. *Proceedings and Reports,* For the Year Ending September 30, 1927, p. 17.
[42]Ibid., p. 17.

dormitory and teachers' home; the principal's house, and several small frame structures which were erected by the boys in the manual training courses. These buildings house farm machinery, cattle, pigs, chickens, etc.

A staff of five teachers and the principal conduct the educational offerings in the secondary grades. One of these teachers is the "Smith-Hughes teacher," who has charge of the industrial and agricultural work conducted in the school and in the neighboring county. The student body approximates 300 persons, of whom about half are found in the high school grades. This secondary enrollment is somewhat higher than that usually found in a Training School of this size. The main building has a large auditorium, which seats 350 persons comfortably. A fine secondary school library is also housed in this building. The work of the school is fully accredited by the State Department of Education.

Some idea of the school-community relationship can be sensed from the following account of this type of activity. Prior to 1929, the Negroes in this county raised largely cotton and tobacco crops. When the depression set in, few of these farmers re-directed their efforts toward producing crops which would be of use in daily living. With the cotton and tobacco markets virtually closed to them much poverty and suffering resulted. In 1929 Mr. Cheek, principal of the school, with his staff and others, initiated a campaign to persuade Negro farmers to raise corn, wheat, cattle, pigs, and chickens on a scale large enough to supply the Negro citizenry with food. Sufficient money was raised to purchase modern farm machinery. This was sent out from the School and used cooperatively by the farmers. The first year three families raised 300 bushels of wheat between them. Three years later 125 families raised 4,500 bushels of wheat. One Negro started a flour mill. Negro farmers now cooperate in using this machinery and do much corn-cutting, threshing, etc., for white farmers. With the money raised, they have purchased a pedigreed bull, several fine breeding hogs, and fine Leghorn and Rhode Island Red chicken breeders. All are kept at the school and tended by students. All are used cooperatively by the farmers. Adult classes are offered at the school, and garden and poultry projects are conducted by students at their homes. From what has been described it can be seen that this school is, literally, the farm center for the county.

The Montgomery County Training School, Waugh, Alabama

This county is inhabited by 98,000 persons, of whom 52,000 are Negroes. Two schools in Montgomery (City) offer two years of high school work to Negroes. The County Training School is the only one in the entire county offering four years of secondary work. Little or no transportation is provided.

This school is located in the open country, with the surrounding area populated almost entirely by Negroes, and is about twelve miles from the nearest city, Montgomery. Four frame buildings constitute the major portion of the physical plant. This plant consists of the main school building, the domestic and vocational science building, and two frame dwellings occupied by the teaching staff and boarding students. The grounds have been nicely landscaped and are clean and well-kept. The main drive has been named after Dr. Dillard, former president of the Slater Fund, and Lambert Walk has been named for one of the present State Agents for Negro Education. The buildings have no central heating plants, no running water, and all toilet facilities are out-of-doors. Electricity is supplied by a plant on the grounds, which was secured through the cooperative efforts of the Negroes themselves. Several smaller sheds and buildings house farm implements, cattle, pigs, chickens and mules. Several acres of gardens and fields are part of the school property.

The school is organized on the 6-3-3 plan, and has enrolled 325 pupils, of whom 85 are in the secondary grades. The principal, who holds the M.A. degree from Harvard, and three additional teachers provide the instruction in the secondary grades. The school is accredited for three of the four years of high school work that is offered. One senses a fine attitude of cooperation about this school. Modern progressive techniques are employed, especially in the lower elementary grades. Here, however, general over-crowding prevails and limits the extent to which these techniques can be applied.

All the girls wear colored cotton dresses, which have been made in the domestic science classes. This is not designed as an attempt to provide uniforms, but rather as a matter of practical economy both for school use and in the home. The material is durable, washable, inexpensive and not easily soiled. Adult women attend classes and learn, among other things, to make these dresses.

At the time the writer visited the school the "Smith-Hughes teacher" was conducting a class in Biology. A practical lesson was in session. A pig, raised at the school, had just been slaughtered by the boys, under the guidance of their instructor. In a short time they were joined by the girls of the class and the entire group proceeded to study the animal. The teacher used every opportunity to have each member of the group participate in this real-laboratory situation wherein the details of external and internal bodily structure and the functions of certain organs of a mammal could be studied more effectively than would have been possible in an ordinary class-room.

After the boys had attended to the details of cutting and dressing the pig, the girls aided in cleaning and preparing the utensils to be used in making lard, sausages, etc. Throughout the entire project it was obvious that the instructor was using this common-place rural activity,—conducted in a practical, sanitary, and economical manner,—as a medium for vitalized learning.

These two examples are illustrative of County Training Schools which have been thus identified for ten or more years.

Development of County Training Schools in South 49

The success of their work is largely a reflection of wise administrative guidance on the part of the principal and local and state officials. The Slater Fund has played a minor part in providing stimulative funds and, in the earlier history of these schools, some advisory assistance.

The final example to be submitted concerns a school in an early developmental stage. It is indicative of many County Training Schools in their formative stages.

The Spotsylvania County Training School, Snell, Virginia

This county is inhabited by 10,000 persons, of whom 3,000 are Negroes. In addition, it should be mentioned that the population of Fredericksburg city, which has a political autonomy entirely separate from that of the county, aggregates 7,000 persons, of whom 1,200 are Negroes. The Mayfield High School is located in this city and offers four years of secondary work to Negroes.

The Spotsylvania County Training School is fifty-odd miles from Washington, D. C. The school was formerly owned by a Board representing several denominational interests. It has been turned over to the county. In addition to the solitary building, the school grounds include 250 acres of land, much of which is covered with timber. The building is a crude, frame, barnlike structure containing a basement and two floors. Six rooms on the first floor are used for classrooms, and the second floor serves as living quarters for the teaching staff and several boarding students from Louisa county. There is no central heating plant, each room being supplied with a small "cannonball" stove; no electricity; no running water; and a single outside toilet serves the entire school. The grounds and building quite obviously needed renovating.

The school offers four years of high school work, and of the 200 pupils 48 were enrolled in the secondary grades. One part-time teacher and two full-time teachers present the high school subjects. The science equipment represents the bare minimum essentials. There were too few seats for the pupils, and very few text books and supplies seemed to be available for student use. There was no "Smith-Hughes teacher" placed in this school and consequently no agricultural work was offered. The principal, Mr. Duncan, is a graduate of Tuskegee Institute, Alabama, and, while able to offer the manual training, could not teach the agricultural courses. It was the principal's first year at this school. He was working hard to secure community interest and cooperation, and reported that his greatest obstacle was to overcome the lack of parental interest in the work of the school. He was trying to raise $200 in order to bring the school library up to the standards set by the state. The work of this school is not accredited.

These examples are not entirely representative of County

Training Schools wherever they are found. They do, however, give some concrete factual information which should facilitate more intelligent appreciation of what these schools are and how they function. In the last example it should be seen that much remains to be accomplished in bringing this school to a satisfactory status.

A final caution is necessary for those who are not familiar with Negro schools as they are found in the Southern states. There are some splendidly equipped and well staffed schools for Negroes in the South. Unfortunately they constitute a far too inadequate minority and are too largely available only to an urban population. The great majority of Negroes must resort to far less impressive educational agencies than those just mentioned. Frame buildings, frequently outmoded and worn-out, without central heating plants, without running water, without electricity, and with outside toilet accommodations are the rule.[43] County Training Schools are no exceptions to this general type, except that they are usually larger and somewhat better equipped.[44] Schools offering elementary work are invariably badly over-crowded, especially in the first three grades. There is an appalling dearth of text books, and many of those in use are in poor condition or poorly adapted to the students who are supposed to use them.[45] The same scarcity applies to teaching materials. Both of these insufficiencies are due largely to the fact that the majority of Southern states do not supply these items free of charge. When it is recalled that the South as a whole compares unfavorably with the per capita wealth of other sections of the United States, a further reason is seen for this educational poverty. And in these Southern states, the Negro, more often than not, is the poorest of the poor. Finally, one must bear in mind the fact that in the allocation of public monies for educational purposes, a discrimination is practiced to the disadvantage of the Negro, which is exceedingly adroit, if not downright dishonest.[46]

---

[43]Caliver, Ambrose. *Secondary Education for Negroes*, pp. 116-117.
[44]See Chapter IV, section on *State Recognition of County Training Schools*.
[45]Caliver, Ambrose. *Rural Elementary Education Among Negroes Under Jeanes Supervising Teachers*. U. S. Bureau of Education Bulletin, 1933, No. 5, Government. Printing Office, Washington, D. C., pp. 53-57.
[46]McCuistion, Fred. *Financing Schools in the South*, 1930, pp. 16-18; 20; 24-26.
Committee on Finance of the National Conference on Fundamental Problems in the Education of Negroes, (Fred McCuistion, Chairman). *School Money in Black and White*, Published by the Julius Rosenwald Fund, Nashville, Tenn., 1934, pp. 1-22.

Chapter III

THE PRESENT STATUS OF PUBLIC SECONDARY EDUCATION FOR NEGROES

BEFORE any attempt could be made to determine the extent to which County Training Schools are a factor in public Negro secondary education, it was necessary to secure information which would indicate the present status of this field. This chapter attempts to present a more nearly complete statement about the provision of public secondary educational facilities than has been available hitherto.

THE NEGRO POPULATION IN THE SOUTHERN STATES

A study of the Census returns for 1930 indicates that there were, at that time, 9,586,000 Negroes living in the District of Columbia and the seventeen Southern states maintaining separate schools for Negro and white children. This number represented 81 per cent of the total Negro population in continental United States. Of these Negroes, 1,081,600 were adolescents between the ages of 15 and 19 years, representing, roughly, the potential secondary school population residing in the Southern states. The next phase of this study is concerned with ascertaining how much secondary education is offered for this group.

THE NUMBER OF SCHOOLS

How many public secondary schools are there for Negro educables in the states maintaining dual systems? Are they located in rural or urban communities? How many years of secondary work do they offer? How many fully accredited four-year public secondary schools are there? The answers to these questions on numerical status, distribution, and types of schools are indicated in Table V.

Data on private secondary schools[1] were not collected for this study and, consequently, Table V presents information concerning public secondary schools only. This, however, is almost

---

[1] In 1929-30 only 9,868 pupils in Negro private secondary schools were reported to the United States Office of Education. Caliver reported 112 private schools in 15 Southern states, 94 of which were accredited.

TABLE V

PUBLIC SECONDARY SCHOOLS FOR NEGROES IN SEVENTEEN SOUTHERN STATES AND THE DISTRICT OF COLUMBIA, 1932-33, CLASSIFIED ACCORDING TO RURAL AND URBAN DISTRIBUTION†

State	Number of Schools Offering 4 Years of Work		Number of Secondary Schools by Years of Work Offered and Location										Total
	Accredited	Total	Rural					Urban					
			One	Two	Three	Four	Total	One	Two	Three	Four	Total	
Alabama	5	51	47	5	6	40	98	11	13	2	11	37	135
Arkansas	15	18	20	12	7	5	44	8	8	3	13	32	76
Delaware	2	2	2	...	2	...	4	...	...	...	2	2	6
Florida	9	32	9	3	...	3	15	4	10	1	29	44	59
Georgia	14	54	46	62	27	27	162	5	9	3	27	44	206
Kentucky	38	49	1	12	8	13	34	3	2	3	36	44	78
Louisiana	3**	41	4	7	6	15	32	2	2	5	26	35	67
Maryland	25	25	...	2	...	9	11	3	1	...	16	20	31
Mississippi	1*	30	30	43	11	14	98	3	4	7	16	30	128
Missouri	14	22	1	2	2	5	10	...	8	1	17	26	36
North Carolina	99	126	13	31	26	80	150	2	1	2	46	51	201
Oklahoma	25	55	1	6	9	32	48	1	1	...	23	24	72
South Carolina	3	47	81	51	49	23	204	1	5	7	24	37	241
Tennessee	28	39	1	16	4	14	35	...	10	5	25	40	75
Texas	35	122	74	106	98	46	324	12	11	21	76	120	444
Virginia	28	62	5	11	16	48	80	...	4	1	14	19	99
West Virginia	20	29	5	4	...	14	23	3	...	...	15	18	41
District of Columbia	3	3	...	...	...	...	...	5	...	...	3	8	8
TOTAL	367	807	340	373	271	388	1,372	62	89	61	419	631	2,003

*There are 22 other schools approved by Mr. P. H. Easom, the State Agent for Negro Education. This approval means that they are attempting to do 4 years' work but not meeting accrediting requirements. The approval rating gives colleged some idea of how to admit students who undertake to enter college.

**There are 37 other schools approved by the State on a little lower level than accredited schools.

†Tables V to XVII inclusive were compiled from data which were secured from questionnaires sent to superintendents of schools in the states included in the study. The data and their sources are explained in detail in Chapter II.

Present Status of Public Negro Secondary Education 53

complete. Any omissions which might prevail would be confined largely to a few schools offering one or two years of secondary work to relatively few students and would usually involve one or two-teacher elementary schools in rural locations. There were not less than 2,003 public secondary schools for Negroes in the states included in this investigation in 1933. One thousand three hundred seventy-two of these schools are located in rural places and 631 are found in urban centers. Since 67.4 per cent of the Negro population of these states is rural, and 69 per cent of all secondary schools are located in rural communities, the division seems consistent. Some interesting tendencies are revealed, however, when this rural-urban distribution of schools is studied more closely.

In addition to showing all the secondary schools classified with respect to the number of years of work offered, Table VI also makes possible a comparison of the proportionate number of the four types of schools found in rural and urban localities.

TABLE VI
DISTRIBUTION OF SCHOOLS ACCORDING TO NUMBER OF YEARS OF SECONDARY WORK OFFERED

Type of School by Location	Type of School by Years of Work Offered				
	1-Year	2-Year	3-Year	4-Year	Total
All Schools Reporting					
Number	402	462	332	807	2,003
Per cent	20.1	23.1	16.6	40.2	100.0
Rural High Schools					
Number	340	373	271	388	1,372
Per cent	24.8	27.2	19.7	28.3	100.0
Urban High Schools					
Number	62	89	61	419	631
Per cent	9.8	14.1	9.7	66.4	100.0

Only 40.2 per cent of the Negro secondary schools offered four years' work, and the majority offered amounts varying from one to three years. Of the schools operating in rural and small population centers, but 28.3 per cent offered four years of secondary work, and 52 per cent offered two years or less. On the other hand, an analysis of the distribution of urban schools reveals that 66.4 per cent offered four years of secondary work, and 23.9 per cent provided two years or less. Looking at the comparison in another way, it may be seen from Table VII

TABLE VII
Proportion of Schools, by Years of Secondary Work Offered, Located in Rural and Urban Communities

Type of School by Location	Percentage of Schools Offering			
	1 Year	2 Years	3 Years	4 Years
Rural High Schools...............	84.6	80.7	81.6	48.1
Urban High Schools............	15.4	19.3	18.4	51.9

that 84.6 per cent of all one-year, 80.7 per cent of all two-year and 81.6 per cent of all three-year secondary schools were located in rural communities. Thus it is seen that, in so far as the Negro secondary schools are concerned, certain educational problems are confined, by and large, to those rural schools offering less than a four-year secondary course. It is seen, also, that but 48.1 per cent of the public four-year secondary schools were in rural places although 67.4 per cent of the total Negro population lives in rural localities.

The Accredited Secondary Schools

An interesting feature of Table V is the number of accredited four-year secondary schools available to 148,754 Negro high school pupils enrolled in the 2,003 schools considered in this investigation. Three hundred sixty-seven of the 807 four-year secondary schools have been accredited by the authorities in State Departments of Education. Thirty-nine of these state accredited schools have also been placed upon the accredited list of the Southern Association of Colleges and Secondary Schools;[2] six have been accredited by the Middle States Association of Colleges and Secondary Schools; and two are included in the list of the North Central Association of Colleges and Secondary Schools. Of the total number of students enrolled in all public Negro secondary schools 79,265, or 53.3 per cent, were found in the 367 accredited four-year high schools. The fact that 224 of these accredited schools are located in urban communities indicates a further unfavorable distribution of secondary educational opportunity for rural high school students.

It should be mentioned that wide differences in methods and standards for accrediting exist among the several states. In all but three states, secondary schools for Negroes are accredited

[2] Listed as of December 8, 1933.

on the same basis as schools for whites.³ There is a tendency among the several states to accredit the larger schools, and standards reflect the familiar characteristics of the more privileged urban schools. Some indication of the wide differences in practices and standards employed in accrediting is at least partially reflected in the numbers of such schools listed by states. Florida, Louisiana, Mississippi, and South Carolina reported a total of but sixteen public Negro secondary schools fully accredited for four-year work in 1933. All are located in large urban centers. On the other hand, North Carolina had accredited ninety-nine secondary schools for Negroes, which were almost equally distributed with respect to rural and urban location.

An important phase of this investigation involved an extensive field trip wherein visits to many schools were made in order to secure knowledge of use in the interpretation of data, and to assist in validating conclusions. The outstanding impression gained was that certain states, such as Louisiana and South Carolina, possessed unaccredited secondary schools which compared favorably with accredited schools in other states, such as North Carolina and Virginia. Similar comparisons would hold good for other states.

This is not a criticism of the accrediting standards in any one state. It does reflect, in a measure, the attitude of certain states toward the general problem of accrediting public secondary schools for Negroes.

It is generally conceded that the fundamental purpose of accrediting is to improve the quality of educational offering. Students attending such schools, in general, should be better prepared to continue their education in higher institutions than those attending unaccredited schools. As Negro educational authorities[4] are urging greater selectivity in admissions in order to reduce the large number of poorly prepared students who enter, the number of Negro students enrolled in accredited schools is highly important. If selection is to be exercised, then a sufficient number of subjects to make it feasible must be available.

---

[3] Robinson, W. A. "Four-Year State Accredited High Schools for Negroes in the South, *Bulletin of the National Association of Teachers in Colored Schools*. Vol. VIII, 1928. pp. 15-16.
[4] Caliver, Ambrose. *A Background Study of Negro College Students*, pp. 104, 112.

In a study of representative public and private schools in the Southern states it was reported that of those who enroll in Negro secondary schools, only 8.6 per cent remain to graduate.[5] Thirty-five per cent of these graduates continue their education in some college or university.[6]

Since the author was unable to ascertain how many of the 9,868 Negro secondary pupils who were enrolled in the 112 private schools were in the 94 schools which were accredited,[7] the entire number was added to the 79,265 pupils who were reported as being enrolled in public accredited schools in 1933. For purposes of the discussion which follows it can reasonably be assumed that 89,133 would include all Negro secondary pupils who were in accredited high schools in the South in 1933. Using this number and on the basis of 8.6 per cent, about 7,600 Negro secondary pupils could be expected to be graduated by the accredited schools. Of this number, 35 per cent, or approximately 2,660 students, could be expected to go on to college.

A recent study of 112 out of 118 public and private Negro colleges and universities reported 9,461 students enrolled in the Freshman class.[8] Of this number approximately three-quarters came from non-southern states.[9] When the number of those admitted to higher institutions is more than double the number graduated by the better secondary schools it is obvious that the problem of selective admissions has a direct relationship to the number of accredited schools. As things stand now it is likely that the better higher institutions will be able to exercise some selection, while the remainder will have to be far less selective until the general level of secondary schools for Negroes is raised. Seen from the point of view of college entrance, it should be desirable to encourage Negro secondary schools to meet accrediting requirements. On the other hand, it is equally desirable that schools be adequately adapted to meet the needs of the vast majority who do not go on to higher institutions.

---

[5]Caliver, Ambrose. *Secondary Education for Negroes*, p. 56.
[6] *Ibid.* pp. 59-60.
[7] *Ibid.*, pp. 14, 26.
[8] The John F. Slater Fund. *Proceedings and Reports.* For the Year Ending June 30, 1934, pp. 16-21.
[9]Caliver, Ambrose. Op. cit., p. 10.

Present Status of Public Negro Secondary Education

There is nothing necessarily inherent in the function of accrediting to prevent the realization of all secondary educational objectives.

THE SECONDARY ENROLLMENT[10]

Comparative facts regarding the enrollment in public Negro secondary schools are shown in Table VIII.

TABLE VIII
NUMBER OF SCHOOLS, ENROLLMENT AND NUMBER OF TEACHERS IN PUBLIC SECONDARY SCHOOLS FOR NEGROES IN SEVENTEEN SOUTHERN STATES AND THE DISTRICT OF COLUMBIA, 1932-1933

Type of School by Years of Work Offered	Number of Schools			Secondary Enrollment			Number of Secondary School Teachers		
	Rural	Urban	Total	Rural	Urban	Total	Full Time	Part Time	Total
1-Year	340	62	402	2,784	3,915	6,699	196	359	555
2-Year	373	89	462	6,344	2,667	9,011	327	354	681
3-Year	271	61	332	7,960	4,665	12,625	448	215	663
4-Year	388	419	807	30,662	89,757	120,419	4,327	550	4,877
Total	1,372	631	2,003	47,750	101,004	148,754	5,298	1,478	6,776

While the 1,372 rural secondary schools constitute 69 per cent of all high schools reported, only 32.1 per cent of the total secondary enrollment is found in the rural schools. It was previously indicated in Table VI that 60 per cent of the rural schools offered less than four years' work. On the other hand, the remaining 631 urban schools accommodate 67.9 per cent of the total number of Negro secondary students. Sixty-six per cent of the urban schools offered four years of high school work. More than half of all four-year secondary schools are located in urban communities. While a few of the most progressive counties in several of the Southern states are providing transportation or providing board and room at reasonable prices,[11] relatively little has been done to make secondary schools accessible to the constituency they are intended to serve.[12] When this fact is associated with the observation that 67.4 per cent of the total Negro population is rural, these figures have a further implication. The disproportionate ratio proves that the general availability

---

[10] Appendix B includes complete state-by-state compilations of facts pertaining to numbers of schools, the enrollment, number of teachers in 1-year, 2-year, 3-year and 4-year public secondary schools.
[11] Long, Hollis M. *Secondary Education for Negroes in North Carolina*, p. 28.
[12] Caliver, Ambrose. *Secondary Education for Negroes*, pp. 34-37.

of secondary facilities for Negroes is tremendously in favor of the urban dweller.

The enrollment that would correspond to the four years or grades included in the public secondary schools for Negroes in the South is shown in Table IX.

TABLE IX
PUBLIC NEGRO SECONDARY SCHOOL ENROLLMENT BY YEARS IN SEVENTEEN SOUTHERN STATES AND THE DISTRICT OF COLUMBIA, 1932-33

State	Secondary Enrollment by Years				Total	Per cent 4th Year is of Total
	First	Second	Third	Fourth		
Alabama	3,454	2,224	1,686	1,372	8,736	15.7
Arkansas	1,512	1,005	625	466	3,608	12.9
Delaware	309	235	190	112	846	13.3
Florida	1,952	1,463	1,033	758	5,206	14.6
Georgia	4,477	2,694	1,870	1,330	10,371	12.8
Kentucky	1,873	1,383	1,031	819	5,106	16.0
Louisiana	2,922	2,042	1,358	1,197	7,519	15.9
Maryland	2,129	1,376	978	765	5,248	14.6
Mississippi	2,603	1,763	1,026	586	5,978	9.8
Missouri	1,934	1,331	928	716	4,909	14.5
North Carolina	9,143	6,095	4,438	3,369	23,045	14.6
Oklahoma	2,005	1,616	1,275	994	5,890	16.9
South Carolina	4,576	2,812	1,975	1,206	10,569	11.4
Tennessee	2,823	2,682	1,779	1,355	8,659	15.6
Texas	8,231	6,124	4,426	3,800	22,581	16.8
Virginia	4,612	3,091	2,217	1,510	11,430	13.2
West Virginia	1,471	1,045	737	617	3,870	15.9
Dist of Columbia	1,749	1,582	996	856	5,183	16.5
TOTAL	57,775	40,573	28,578	21,828	148,754	
Per cent of total	38.8	27.2	19.3	14.7	100.0	

At this time no intensive comparison by states would be expedient. It should be noted, however, that 38.8 per cent of those pupils who survived the elementary school and enrolled in secondary schools were found in the first high school year. Only 14.7 per cent of the total were in the last year. This decrease in percentage represents the approximate elimination which takes place. The percentage of secondary enrollment in the fourth year varies considerably. Mississippi with 9.8 per cent stands at one extreme, while Oklahoma with 16.9 per cent is at the other.

Some indication of the relation the secondary school enrollment bears to the approximated Negro population of high school age is indicated in Table X.

TABLE X
PERCENTAGE OF NEGROES 15 TO 19 YEARS OF AGE[13] ENROLLED IN PUBLIC SECONDARY SCHOOLS IN 1932-33

State	Negro Population 15 to 19 Years of Age Total in State	Per cent Enrolled in High Schools	State	Negro Population 15 to 19 Years of Age Total in State	Per cent Enrolled in High Schools
Delaware	2,985	28.3	Arkansas	52,545	6.9
West Virginia	10,109	38.2	Virginia	73,443	15.6
Dist. of Columbia	10,675	48.5	Louisiana	81,293	9.2
Missouri	17,735	27.7	Texas	92,696	24.4
Oklahoma	18,811	31.3	South Carolina	105.429	9.9
Kentucky	20,762	24.6	Alabama	109,216	8.0
Maryland	25,417	20.7	Mississippi	114,893	5.2
Florida	43,355	12.0	North Carolina	115,166	20.0
Tennessee	51,835	16.7	Georgia	134,216	7.7

Of the total group between the ages of 15 and 19 years 13.7 per cent was enrolled in public secondary schools. This means that about 932,800 Negroes of high school age were *not* enrolled in public secondary schools. To be sure, some of these were in private schools, and a relatively small number were in the elementary grades.

Among the states listed, West Virginia, Delaware, and Oklahoma show the highest percentages of Negroes 15 to 19 years of age enrolled. On the other hand, Mississippi, Arkansas, Georgia, Alabama, Louisiana and South Carolina enrolled less than ten per cent of their respective potential secondary pupils.

The relationship existing between the percentage enrolled and the total number of Negroes of secondary age may be seen in Table X. The extent to which these factors go together is indicated by the coefficient of correlation of —.79 ± .06. This correlation indicates that there is a decided tendency for the percentage enrolled in the secondary schools to be higher in states possessing the fewer Negroes of high school age and vice versa. One might be led to think that this relationship is more or less inevitable but it is seen from Table X that Arkansas (6.9 per cent) and Florida (12 per cent) are exceptions since they have smaller Negro populations. North Carolina (20 per cent) and Texas (24.4 per cent), on the other hand, are exceptions to the relationship indicated above since their Negro populations are very large.

[13] All population data used in this study were taken from the U. S. Census of 1930.

THE SIZE OF NEGRO SECONDARY SCHOOLS

The distribution of public secondary schools according to size of enrollments is shown in Table XI. By giving the per cent in the enrollment range, and grouping the schools in intervals of twenty and fifty pupils, it gives a general view of the entire situation.

TABLE XI
DISTRIBUTION OF PUBLIC SECONDARY SCHOOLS FOR NEGROES IN SEVENTEEN SOUTHERN STATES AND THE DISTRICT OF COLUMBIA, 1932-33, ACCORDING TO SIZE OF ENROLLMENT

Type of School	Distribution by Size of Enrollment										
	20 or less	21 to 40	41 to 60	61 to 80	81 to 100	101 to 150	151 to 200	201 to 250	251 to 300	301 or More	Total
All High Schools Reporting:											
Number	787	393	228	139	102	149	78	34	15	78	2,003
Per cent	39.3	19.6	11.4	6.9	5.1	7.4	3.9	1.7	.8	3.9	100.0
All Rural High Schools Reporting:											
Number	696	295	149	84	50	62	18	9	3	6	1,372
Per cent	50.7	21.5	10.9	6.1	3.7	4.5	1.3	.7	.2	.4	100.0
All Urban High Schools Reporting:											
Number	91	98	79	55	52	87	60	25	12	72	631
Per cent	14.4	15.5	12.5	8.8	8.4	13.5	9.5	4.0	1.9	11.5	100.0

Considering first the distribution of all schools, it is apparent that 70.3 per cent of the public Negro secondary schools enrolled sixty or fewer pupils; 82.3 per cent had enrollments of less than 101 pupils; and but 3.9 per cent enrolled more than 300 students. Less than 2 per cent of the high schools in rural areas enrolled more than 200 pupils. Slightly more than 42 per cent of the 631 schools functioning in urban centers had enrollments smaller than 61 pupils per school, whereas 83.1 per cent of the 1,372 rural schools indicated enrollments per school below this figure.

The data point overwhelmingly to the conclusion that Negro schools offering public secondary education are small in size as measured by enrollment.

Table XII shows the comparison in a somewhat different manner. As the size of enrollment increases in schools located in rural areas, the percentage of the total number of schools in a particular size-group decreases. Urban schools, however, re-

TABLE XII
PROPORTION OF EACH SIZE GROUP LOCATED IN RURAL AND URBAN COMMUNITIES

Type of School by Location	Percentages Enrolling								
	20 or less	21 to 40	41 to 60	61 to 80	81 to 100	101 to 150	151 to 200	201 to 250	251 to 300	301 or More
Rural High Schools	88.5	75.0	65.4	60.4	49.0	41.6	23.1	26.5	20.0	7.7
Urban High Schools	11.5	25.0	34.6	39.6	51.0	58.4	76.9	73.5	80.0	92.3

veal a relationship in size in the reverse order. Thus it is that 88.5 per cent of all schools enrolling twenty or fewer pupils are found in rural places. At the other end of the scale, 92.3 per cent of all schools enrolling more than 300 pupils are found in urban centers.

By turning to Table XIII, the different types of schools grouped according to enrollment range and location may be seen.

TABLE XIII
DISTRIBUTION OF PUBLIC SECONDARY SCHOOLS FOR NEGROES IN SEVENTEEN SOUTHERN STATES AND THE DISTRICT OF COLUMBIA, ACCORDING TO ENROLLMENT, 1932-33

Enrollment	Number of Schools								Total
	1-Year		2-Year		3-Year		4-Year		
	Rural	Urban	Rural	Urban	Rural	Urban	Rural	Urban	
1001 and over								16	16
901-1000								2	2
801- 900								3	3
701- 800								4	4
601- 700							1	9	10
501- 600							1	10	11
401- 500							1	14	15
301- 400		4					3	12	19
251- 300		1				1	3	10	15
201- 250		3		2		0	9	20	34
151- 200		6		2		2	18	48	76
101- 150		1	3	4	5	2	54	80	149
81- 100		1	1	4	5	2	44	45	102
61- 80		1	4	4	10	7	70	43	139
41- 60		3	26	7	37	11	86	58	228
21- 40	14	9	89	31	109	21	83	37	393
11- 20	49	8	137	24	82	11	13	6	330
1- 10	277	25	113	11	23	4	2	2	457
Total	340	62	373	89	271	61	388	419	2,003
Mean size	8.2	63.1	17.0	29.9	29.4	76.5	79.0	214.2	74.2
Median size	6.9	12.9	16.4	27.5	26.6	35.8	67.3	109.4	26.5

The distribution begins at one extreme with intervals of one to ten, and ends with schools enrolling more than one thousand pupils. By using narrow intervals in the lower ranges of the distribution, Table XIII reveals clearly the large number of extremely small schools which attempt to offer secondary work. Generally speaking, a rural public secondary school enrolling 200 pupils is considered comparatively large.[14] On the other hand, it is claimed that schools of fewer than 150 pupils do not, usually, render the full service of secondary education.[15] But eighteen of the rural schools enrolled more than two hundred, while 1,330, or 97 per cent of all rural schools, enrolled less than 150 pupils. Referring to the urban schools, those enrolling more than 300 pupils stand on the border line between what are ordinarily classed as small, and those classed as large, secondary schools. Only 70 urban Negro secondary schools enrolled more than 300 pupils. A comparison of the mean and median size as shown in Table XIII further emphasizes the limited size of these schools. Thus it is concluded that Negro secondary schools, regardless of location, are small schools. Unless consolidation and transportation is practiced to an extent apparently unlikely, these schools will remain small. Obviously then, whatever may be the problems inherent in small secondary schools, they also are the problems of practically all public Negro secondary schools. If the child attending the small high school is, in most cases, instructed by a poorly trained and over-burdened teaching staff; and handicapped by a limited, narrow, maladjusted program of educational activities, and by the absence or meagerness of educational equipment then most Negro children attending secondary schools are also sufferers from these conditions.

Undoubtedly many small secondary schools do superior work. On the other hand a large part of the problem hinges on costs. Practically all studies report higher costs in smaller than larger schools, while, at the same time, lower teacher salaries, more limited curriculum offerings, and shorter school terms are the rule in the smaller schools. This factor of higher

---

[14]Gaumnitz, Walter H. *The Smallness of America's Rural High Schools.* United States Bureau of Education Bulletin, 1930, No. 13. Government Printing Office, Washington, D. C., p. 12.
[15]Ferriss, Emery N., Gaumnitz, W. H. and Brammell, Roy P. *The Smaller Secondary Schools.* United States Bureau of Education Bulletin, 1932, No. 17, Monograph No. 6, Government Printing Office, Washington, D. C., p. viii.

costs prevailing in small secondary schools is particularly important in the South where a low per capita wealth prevails.

By and large, the implication is that very small Negro secondary schools should be reduced to the lowest number possible.

THE INSTRUCTIONAL STAFF

The number of teachers and average teaching staff found in the several types of public secondary schools are indicated in Table XIV.

TABLE XIV

NUMBER OF TEACHERS AND AVERAGE TEACHING STAFF AS FOUND IN FOUR TYPES OF PUBLIC SECONDARY SCHOOLS FOR NEGROES IN SEVENTEEN SOUTHERN STATES AND THE DISTRICT OF COLUMBIA, 1932-33

Secondary Teachers	Type of Secondary School				Total
	1-Year	2-Year	3-Year	4-Year	
Total in all Schools:					
Full Time	196	327	448	4,327	5,298
Part Time	359	354	215	550	1,478
Average Teaching Staff per School:					
Full Time	.3	.8	1.4	5.3	
Part Time	.9	.8	.6	.7	

Exactly 6,776 teachers were employed in the 2,003 public secondary schools included in this investigation. Of this number 5,298 teachers devoted their full time to secondary school duties, while 1,478 were occupied part of the time with elementary school duties and the remainder of the time with secondary school work. The rural teachers numbered 2,423 full-time, and 1,152 part-time instructors.

The average number of full-time teachers per school increases as the school offers more years of secondary work and the part-time teachers decrease.

Disregarding any rural-urban differentiation, it is seen that the average teaching staff index of the typical four-year school would be five full-time teachers and one or two part-time instructors. It should be pointed out that many of the full-time teachers reported are also principals of their schools. As such, their time is divided between teaching secondary subjects and the exercise of administrative control over both the elementary and secondary departments. The significance of this is seen when attention is called to the fact that 89 per cent of all Negro secondary schools are essentially elementary schools with one or more years of secondary work included at the top,—often at the expense of the lower school.

Then, too, many "Smith-Hughes teachers" are listed as full-time secondary teachers, even though they spend much of their time in agricultural and industrial extension work in the surrounding communities.

For purposes of general comparison it may be stated that the average public Negro four-year secondary school enrolls 149 pupils and is taught by a staff of six teachers, two of whom devote only part time to the high school subjects. The number of pupils per teacher would approximate 25. This agrees with Favrot's[16] conclusion that Negro high schools generally are not over-crowded.

Reference to Table VI reveals that 84.6 per cent of the one-year secondary schools are in rural localities. Table XIII shows that the mean secondary enrollment per one-year school is eight pupils. If the mean size of urban one-year schools is corrected to allow for the high enrollments in the last year of the junior high schools listed in this category, the mean is but slightly higher than the figure for rural schools. Table XIV indicates that the average one-year school does not command the services of a full-time secondary teacher. The average *total* enrollment of these one-year secondary schools is 140 pupils.[17] Of the rural one-year "secondary" schools *reported*, 90 schools had total enrollments of less than 75 pupils, and 158 enrolled numbers varying between 75 and 150 pupils. Furthermore, it is probable that there are more of the one-year type which, for one reason or another, were not reported by the different county and state officials.

The implications of these facts are both pathetic and extremely serious. In the first place, it appears that the great majority of these rural one-year secondary schools are in reality one and two teacher rural elementary schools trying to satisfy

---

[16] Favrot, Leo M. "Some Facts About Negro High Schools and their Distribution and Development in the Southern States," *High School Quarterly*, Vol. XVII, 1929, pp. 139-154.

[17] Elementary and secondary students.

Present Status of Public Negro Secondary Education 65

the growing educational demands of an under-privileged constituency reaching for secondary educational opportunities. With few exceptions, the two-year secondary schools also are, fundamentally, small rural elementary schools trying to offer something which goes by the name of secondary education. In a sense, it indicates the popularization of secondary education among Negroes, and at the same time suggests the willingness of the Negro to accept whatever secondary facilities are available to him.

This zeal of the rural Negro educator and student does not, however, act for the best interest of the cause of education. It simply causes the veneer of education, already ludicrously thin, to be spread more thinly. The rural Negro elementary schools represent much that is least desirable in the entire American educational system. Herein are found most of the poorest trained and underpaid teachers. It is necessary only to examine these schools to find the shortest terms, the poorest attendance, the meanest equipment and teaching materials, and the crudest buildings serving as school houses.[18] While the motive which prompts educators to stretch the meagre assets they possess may be noble, it is educationally unsound.

ORGANIZATION OF PUBLIC SECONDARY SCHOOLS FOR NEGROES

It is not the purpose of this section of the study to include under *organization*, ". . . all the arrangements which the school makes to furnish a framework for effective education." Rather, interest here centers chiefly in presenting the types of organization found among Negro schools in the several Southern states. Since 1910, secondary schools for children of the majority race have *reorganized* increasingly along junior-senior high school lines. Some conception of the extent to which this movement for reorganization has affected Negro secondary schools will be revealed.

Fifty-eight per cent of the total public Negro secondary population of the South resides in Georgia, Louisiana, Maryland, North Carolina, South Carolina, Texas, and Virginia.

---

[18]Caliver, Ambrose. *Rural Elementary Education Among Negroes Under Jeanes Supervising Teachers*, pp. 53-57.

Except for a few urban systems, all schools within these states have eleven-grade systems with the conventional four-year high school composed of grades 8 through 11. Danville and Roanoke, Virginia, reported twelve-grade systems with the regular 8-4 organization for the elementary and secondary divisions. The only *reorganized* secondary schools for Negroes reported in these states were found in four large city systems. Savannah and Atlanta, Georgia, and Baltimore, Maryland, provide six-year elementary organizations and separate three-year junior and senior high schools. New Orleans, Louisiana, reported a modification of the 7-4 organization, two junior high schools grouping grades 8, 9, and 10 in separate buildings, and one senior high school consisting of grades ten and eleven. The reorganized schools of these seven states enrolled in the junior-senior high school grades 13,951 pupils, of which 5,724 were in the last four secondary grades.

In the ten remaining states included in this study, 12-grade systems prevail, and several variations for the organization of the secondary divisions in Negro schools are employed.

Mississippi, Missouri, Oklahoma, and Tennessee are almost uniformly committed to the conventional 8-4 system for Negro schools, and grades nine through twelve constitute the secondary division. Tulsa, Oklahoma, and Nashville, Tennessee, however, reported the 6-3-3 type of organization.

With the exception of eight schools, Kentucky seems to employ the straight eight-four type of organization. In only two of the eight reorganized school systems, Louisville and Paducah, are separate three-year junior and senior high schools reported. Four of the remaining reorganized schools employ 6-3-3 grade groupings, two use the 6-6 plan, and one reported the 6-2-4 modification.

The majority of Negro secondary students in Delaware attend the high school in Wilmington, where the 6-6 plan of organization is in effect.

Alabama, Florida, and West Virginia have reorganized practically all of the Negro schools in so far as the last six years constitute the secondary grades. The State Departments of Education have adopted uniform programs of studies and standards for the reorganized high school divisions. The ex-

Present Status of Public Negro Secondary Education 67

tent to which actually reorganized procedures have been effected, however, varies both between states and within a given state. The public Negro secondary schools of Florida are mostly located in urban communities and the majority report 6-6 groupings of the grades. In Alabama and West Virginia the schools are about equally divided with respect to rural-urban distribution. In Alabama, while most of the schools reported 6-3-3 organizations, it is certain that few had separate buildings for junior and senior high schools. The movement is state-wide, and most of the schools are just beginning actually to incorporate methods reputed to give the reorganized grouping of grades some educational advantages not likely to result under the conventional scheme. West Virginia schools largely reported the 6-6 type of reorganization.

With the exception of a few schools employing the 8-4 grade organization, the six-year elementary system prevailed in Arkansas in 1933. Reorganized schools were accredited by the State Department as 6-6, 6-3-3, 6-4, and 6-3 types. There were no state high school courses of study, but, in general, an effort was made locally to attempt junior high school programs. The supervision of such programs seemed to be exceedingly limited.

All Negro schools in Washington, D. C., are organized on a six-year elementary basis, with separate three-year junior and senior high schools.

Approximately 71,000 Negro students in the South are enrolled in the *last six* grades of those schools found in reorganizations involving some modification of the six-year secondary school scheme. Except for schools in eighteen or twenty cities, it is extremely doubtful if many other separate three-year junior and senior high schools are to be found. With few exceptions, the secondary schools which are based upon a six-year elementary school are in reality six-year high schools. Many of these schools have failed to incorporate supposedly desirable features concerning articulation, guidance, program of studies, extra-curriculum, and composition of teaching force. These features are supposed to be of vital importance in securing the educational dividends yielded through reorganization. The reorganized Negro schools have adopted, generally, a somewhat more comprehensive and flexible organization than that which characterizes many of the more conventionally organized schools.

Brief mention should be made of the many schools, principally in rural districts, offering two or three years of secondary work and calling themselves "Junior High Schools." This is done often without the sanction of school officials, but not infrequently the use of the term is encouraged by local officials who seek to mollify the demands of the Negroes for more advanced education and, at the same time, avoid antagonizing those members of the majority race who might object to regular high schools for Negroes. Increasingly, however, the several states are causing these schools to conform to standards of an acceptable nature and are organizing regular two-year high schools. These schools, however, are not considered as junior high schools.

PUBLIC SECONDARY EDUCATIONAL PROVISION FOR NEGROES BY COUNTIES

In discussing educational provision for Negroes or any other group of persons, the presence or absence of a school in a given community or area is of prime importance. This is not considered a complete index for purposes of measurement, but that it has value of the first order in any consideration of provision or availability can hardly be denied.

To ascertain those aspects dealing with public educational provision for Negroes with which this study is concerned, each state was separately studied upon a county-by-county basis. In treating this phase of the study original data employed in the investigation were combined with factual information secured from the United States Census for 1930.[19]

Counties Having Little or No Negro Population

A glance at Table XV will expedite the discussion to follow. There are 1,501 counties in the seventeen states, wherein were found 1,070,906 Negro boys and girls ranging from 15 to 19 years of age. In the entire South not more than a score of counties having a Negro population of less than 50 in this

---

[19]Appendix C includes a careful county-by-county analysis of each state, which has been checked by the State Agents for Negro Education. These lists include information on the following: name, approximate location in the state, and number of Negro inhabitants 15 to 19 years of age in each county. The counties also are classified according to the number of years of public secondary education offered and as to the counties having one or more accredited four-year public secondary school.

Present Status of Public Negro Secondary Education 69

TABLE XV
NUMBER OF COUNTIES AND THE NEGRO POPULATION 15 TO 19 YEARS OF AGE IN SEVENTEEN SOUTHERN STATES (U. S. CENSUS, 1930)

State	Number of Counties Having Less Than 50 Negroes 15 to 19 Years of Age	Total Number of Counties in the State	Negro Population 15 to 19 Years of Age
Alabama	1	67	109,216
Arkansas	25	75	52,545
Delaware	0	3	2,985
Florida	0	67	43,355
Georgia	11	159	134,216
Kentucky	46	120	20,762
Louisiana	0	64	81,293
Maryland	1	23	25,417
Mississippi	0	82	114,893
Missouri	74	114	17,735
North Carolina	10	100	115,166
Oklahoma	27	77	18,811
South Carolina	0	46	106,429
Tennessee	25	95	51,835
Texas	117	254	92,696
Virginia	10	100	73,443
West Virginia	26	55	10,109
Total	373	1,501	1,070,906

general secondary age group provided transportation or high school work for these persons in 1933. Consequently 373 counties in this class were definitely located in order to offset any possible misconception regarding the actual number of counties having a considerable Negro population for which some secondary facilities might be provided. The average number of Negroes 15 to 19 years of age per county in the 373 counties was 12.5 persons. This group constituted 4,701 Negroes or .5 per cent of the total number found in the 1,501 counties. Certain of the larger, sparsely settled counties in Arkansas, Missouri, Oklahoma, and Texas, as well as those located in the mountainous sections of Kentucky, Tennessee, and West Virginia accounted for the greater part of this group. Thus it is that attention is centered upon the remaining 1,128 counties and parishes,[20] possessing a considerable Negro constituency.

Counties Providing Less Than Four Years of Public Secondary Education

Some indication of educational provision, as measured by the presence or absence of public secondary facilities in the

[20] The equivalent of the county in Louisiana is the parish.

several counties and states, is presented in Table XVI. It shows, in close juxtaposition, certain facts pertaining to counties entirely without public secondary facilities, counties possessing one or more schools offering less than 4 years' work, those possessing one or more four year public secondary schools, and the approximate Negro secondary population.

Of grave importance is the situation of Negro boys and girls who have no opportunity to attend a public secondary school unless they leave the county in which they reside. There were 190 counties in the 17 Southern states entirely without public secondary facilities in 1933. These counties contained 66,426 Negroes of the estimated secondary school age. They represented 6.2 per cent of the total group of high school age.

Sixty-eight counties offered one year of secondary work to approximately 42,625 Negroes who would be included in the 15 to 19 age group. Counties offering only two years of secondary work numbered 153, and living therein were 81,990 persons, 15 to 19 years of age. It was previously pointed out that the large majority of one and two-year Negro secondary schools are essentially elementary schools and but crudely adapted to offer anything in the way of secondary education. Therefore, one may conclude that 191,039 Negroes of a potential high school age residing in 411 counties have been provided with few if any public secondary schools in the counties wherein their parents reside as citizens.

In addition to the counties already considered, there were 117 counties wherein 83,786 Negro boys and girls resided who had some opportunity to attend a public school offering three years of secondary work.

Five hundred twenty-eight counties in the Southern states offered less than four years of public secondary education for Negroes in 1933. Of the total number of Negro boys and girls 15 to 19 years of age in the Southern states 25.6 per cent, or 274,825, resided in these counties.

When the facts pertaining to the years of public secondary work offered in counties are translated into percentages, a most interesting tendency is revealed. This is shown in Table XVII.

Present Status of Public Negro Secondary Education 71

TABLE XVI
PUBLIC SECONDARY SCHOOL WORK FOR NEGROES OFFERED BY COUNTIES IN SEVENTEEN SOUTHERN STATES IN 1932-33

	0 Years		1 year only		2 years only		3 years only		4 years		Total Negro Population 15-19
State	No. of Counties	Negro Population 15-19 Years	No. of Counties	Negro Population 15-19 Years	No. of Counties	Negro Population 15-19 Years	No. of Counties	Negro Population 15-19 Years	No. of Counties	Negro Population 15-19 Years	Years of Age for State
Alabama	9	3,805	10	10,803	4	5,509	5	5,215	38	83,882	109,216
Arkansas	8	4,562	9	5,163	14	13,322	6	7,371	13	21,876	52,545
Delaware									3	2,985	2,985
Florida	29	6,080	3	1,175	8	3,348	0		27	32,752	43,355
Georgia	30	11,034	16	12,348	34	21,921	18	15,130	50	73,601	134,216
Kentucky	10	829	1	120	13	1,600	10	1,463	40	15,957	20,762
Louisiana	18	12,814	2	1,648	2	831	4	1,704	38	64,296	81,293
Maryland	2	1,002							20	24,412	25,417
Mississippi	16	15,955	10	7,062	21	21,094	9	13,902	26	56,880	114,893
Missouri	8	769			8	681	3	1,714	21	13,889	17,735
North Carolina	2	375	3	573	4	632	6	1,518	75	111,832	115,166
Oklahoma	12	1,248			3	1,063	1	121	34	16,021	18,811
South Carolina			1	898	3	5,326	11	20,292	31	79,913	106,429
Tennessee	15	1,852	1	203	14	2,164	5	1,966	35	45,087	51,835
Texas	7	295	9	512	16	2,167	27	8,418	78	80,238	92,696
Virginia	18	5,349	2	1,895	7	2,183	12	4,972	51	58,709	73,443
West Virginia	6	457	1	225	2	149			20	9,050	10,109
Total	190	66,426	68	42,625	153	81,990	117	83,786	600	791,380	1,070,906
Per Cent of Total Negro Population 15-19 Years in 17 States		6.2		3.9		7.7		7.8		73.9	

Compiled from data which were secured especially for this investigation. See Chapter II for details.

TABLE XVII
PERCENTAGE OF NEGRO POPULATION 15 TO 19 YEARS OF AGE LIVING IN COUNTIES OFFERING LESS THAN FOUR YEARS OF SECONDARY WORK AND THE AVERAGE NUMBER PER COUNTY

Group 1	Negro Population 15 to 19 Years		Group 2	Negro Population 15 to 19 Years	
	Per Cent Living in Counties Offering Less Than 4 Years Work	Average No. per County		Per Cent Living in Counties Offering Less Than 4 Years Work	Average No. per County
N. Carolina	2.7	1,338	Virginia	19.9	816
Maryland	3.9	1,115	Louisiana	20.9	1,270
W. Virginia	8.3	341	Alabama	23.2	1,655
Tennessee	11.9	741	Florida	24.4	647
Texas	11.9	678	S. Carolina	24.9	2,313
Oklahoma	12.9	370	Georgia	45.0	920
Missouri	17.8	423	Mississippi	50.5	1,401
Kentucky	19.3	281	Arkansas	57.9	1,051

By using the total Negro population 15 to 19 years of age living in a given state,[21] it was possible to compute the percentages of such persons living in counties offering less than four years of public secondary work. Arranging the percentages in rank order from the lowest to highest, two groups were formed. Taking cognizance of one or two exceptions, it is still quite evident that, in general, the probabilities in favor of the Negro student having access to a four year secondary school located in the county wherein he resides decrease as the total Negro population in a given state increases.

Counties Providing Four Years of Public Secondary Education

There were 600 counties having at least one public secondary school which offered four years of secondary work in 1933. Of the total Negro population 15 to 19 years of age in the 17 states 73.9 per cent, or 791,380 persons, resided in these counties. Of these counties, 255 had one or more fully accredited four-year school.

Certain limitations in the county-by-county analysis should be mentioned. The mere presence of a secondary school in a county is, at best, only a rough measure of the educational opportunity provided. Transportation is undoubtedly an important factor. However, transportation for Negro high school students is not provided to any great extent.[22]

[21] In states having Counties inhabited by less than 50 Negroes of this age range, both the number of Counties and the population involved were excluded from the State's total.
[22] Alabama, Florida, Georgia, North Carolina, South Carolina, and Texas in 1930 spent the following amounts for the transportation of high school students: White, $5,594,942—Negro, $30,189. The ratio of white children of high school age to Negro is 2 to 1 in these states.
Caliver, Ambrose. *Secondary Education for Negroes*, pp. 23, 112.

Present Status of Public Negro Secondary Education 73

Another factor involves the tremendous variability in the area of counties. Any one of a dozen counties in Florida or South Carolina would be five or six times the area of many found in Georgia, North Carolina and Virginia. The counties in northeastern Texas are small in size when compared with many in the western part of the state. Other states would yield similar comparisons.

Add to these considerations the lack of sympathetic cooperation between urban centers possessing high schools and less fortunate neighboring rural areas, and it becomes certain that there is less opportunity to secure the secondary level of education than the county-by-county analysis indicates.

Chapter IV

THE PLACE OF COUNTY TRAINING SCHOOLS IN THE PUBLIC NEGRO SECONDARY FIELD

ONE of the most important recent developments in Negro Education has been the growth of County Training Schools, made possible by the cooperation of the county school authorities and the John F. Slater Fund."[1]

The purpose of this chapter is to present evidence which will enable one to determine, as accurately as possible, the place held by these schools in the field of public secondary education for Negroes.

THE COUNTY TRAINING SCHOOLS AIDED BY THE SLATER FUND IN 1932-33

Some conception of the extent of the county training school movement can be obtained by studying certain facts pertaining to the schools assisted by the Slater Fund during a given year. Table XVIII presents this information for the school year, 1932-33.

During 1933, 356 schools located in 352 counties in 14 Southern states were partially subsidized. More than 170,000 pupils were enrolled, and of this number 16,389 were in the secondary grades. The entire teaching force aggregated 2,601 persons, and 936 devoted their full time to the secondary subjects. The remainder were employed in the elementary grades. Therefore, 11 per cent of all Negro children who were enrolled in the public secondary schools in 17 states were attending County Training Schools aided during 1933. They were taught by 17.7 per cent of all Negro teachers in the South devoting full time to high school subjects.

The percentage of a state's total public Negro secondary enrollment found in County Training Schools varied greatly from state to state. Louisiana with 26.8 per cent and Mississippi with 23.7 per cent represent one extreme; Missouri and

---

[1] Caliver, Ambrose. *Secondary Education for Negroes*, p. 33.

TABLE XVIII
SECONDARY ENROLLMENT, NUMBER OF TEACHERS, AND NUMBER OF COUNTY TRAINING SCHOOLS AIDED BY THE JOHN F. SLATER FUND IN 1932-33

State	Number of Schools	Number of H. S. Teachers	Secondary Enrollment	
			In County Training Schools	Per Cent of States's Total
Alabama	31	110	1,428	16.4
Arkansas	21	54	708	19.7
Florida	10	24	207	3.9
Georgia	41	90	1,383	13.3
Kentucky	19	32	564	11.1
Louisiana	28	94	2,019	26.8
Mississippi	36	95	1,412	23.7
Missouri	2	6	83	1.7
North Carolina	26	67	1,451	6.3
Oklahoma	5	10	157	2.7
South Carolina	34	81	1,859	17.6
Tennessee	26	82	1,495	17.3
Texas	34	94	1,723	7.7
Virginia	43	97	1,900	16.6
Total	356	936	16,389	

Tables XVIII to XXV inclusive were compiled from data taken from questionnaires which were returned by superintendents of schools in the states included in the study, and from contracts between the Slater Fund and superintendents of schools. See Chapter II for details..

Oklahoma, with 1.7 and 2.7 per cent, respectively, were indicative of the other trend.

A more significant fact than any mentioned previously is the extent to which these schools provide educational opportunities in the several counties wherein they are located. In 205 counties the Training School was, for Negro pupils, the sole source of secondary education at public expense. To Negroes in areas wherein public secondary education borders so closely on non-existence, these schools render a service which is almost beyond measure.

COUNTY TRAINING SCHOOLS: PAST AND PRESENT[2]

By pointing out the geographical spread and the educational range of the County Training School movement, some idea of its importance was obtained. However, any real at-

[2] This study does not include many private secondary schools and public high schools in cities, which have been aided by the Slater Fund. Only those schools aided as "County Training Schools" are included.

tempt to understand the actual place these schools occupy in the public Negro secondary field necessitates consideration of all schools identified with the movement since 1911. Figure 2, graphically shows the distribution of County Training Schools which were aided by the Slater Fund in 1933 and the schools which were assisted in the past. Since 1911, six hundred twelve schools located in 517 counties in 15 Southern states have been aided by the Fund. Some of them have lost their identities as Training Schools. One of the oldest in the United States, that at Hope, Arkansas, was first known as the *Shover School*, then the *Hempstead County Training School,* and is now known as the *H. C. Yerger High School.* On the other hand, one of the most famous Negro schools in the South has always been known as *The Virginia Randolph Training School,* and is located in Henrico county, Virginia. For purposes of comparison, attention should be directed toward the County Training Schools and their background of the total public Negro secondary field.

Distribution of County Training Schools

Grouped according to geographical distribution, type of school, and the years of secondary work offered, these schools are represented in Table XIX.

TABLE XIX
Distribution of County Training Schools in Fifteen Southern States, 1911-1933

State	1 Year Rural	1 Year Urban	2 Years Rural	2 Years Urban	3 Years Rural	3 Years Urban	4 Years Rural	4 Years Urban	Total
Alabama	1	..	3	1	3	..	35	1	44
Arkansas	7	2	6	5	4	2	2	8	36
Florida	1	1	5	2	..	..	..	14	23
Georgia	4	1	13	6	6	1	20	13	64
Kentucky	..	..	7	1	4	1	11	20	44
Louisiana	1	1	..	..	2	1	13	19	37
Maryland	..	..	..	..	..	..	1	1	2
Mississippi	2	..	18	2	4	6	11	11	54
Missouri	..	..	..	..	..	..	1	2	3
North Carolina	1	..	1	1	4	1	44	27	79
Oklahoma	..	..	1	..	1	..	6	3	11
South Carolina	4	1	7	1	16	3	13	14	59
Tennessee	..	..	3	2	1	3	10	15	34
Texas	2	..	1	..	9	2	22	18	54
Virginia	2	..	7	1	13	1	41	3	68
Total	25	6	72	22	67	21	230	169	612
Per Cent	80.7	..	76.6	..	76.1	..	57.6	..	..

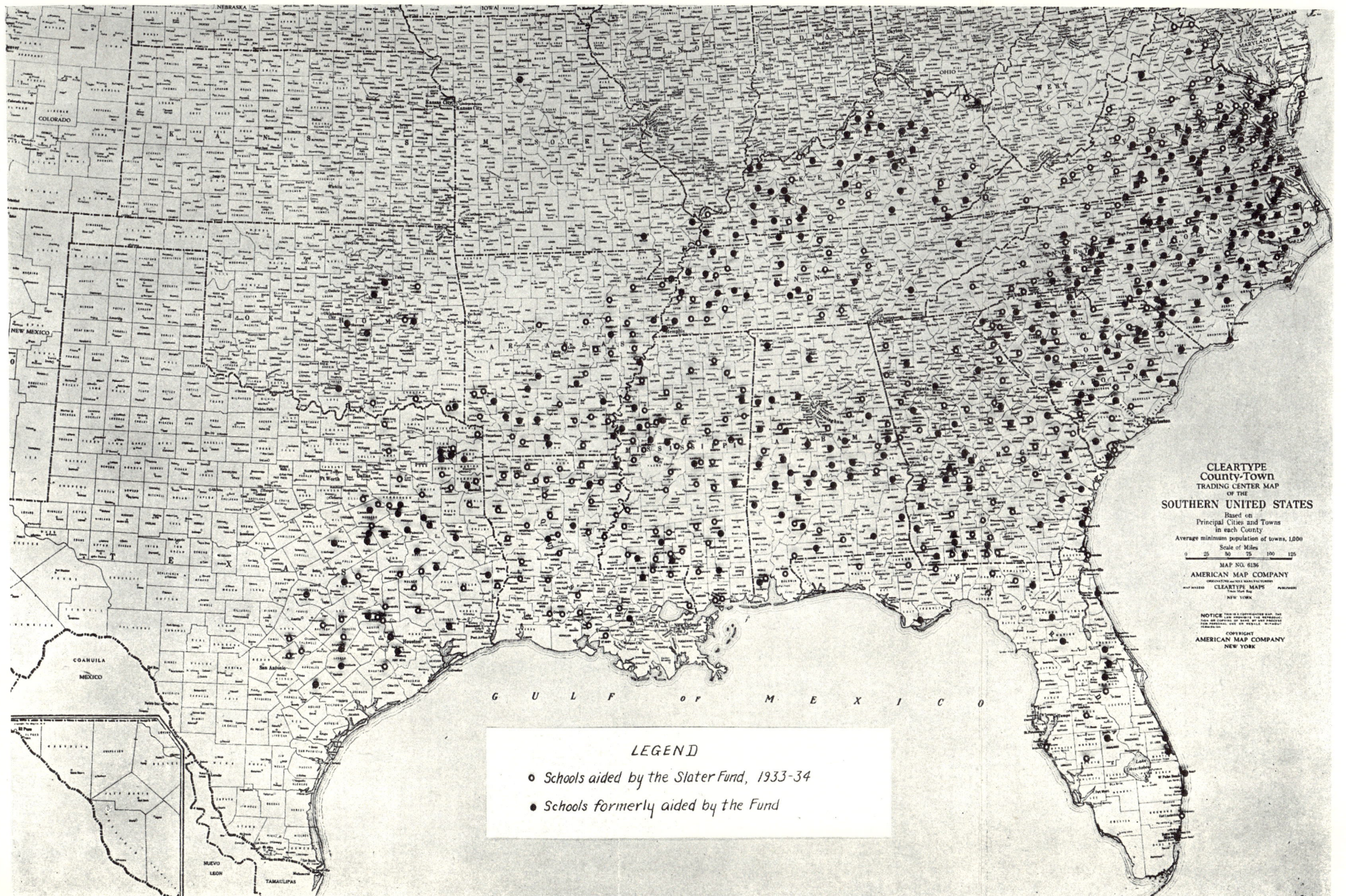

FIGURE 2—DISTRIBUTION OF COUNTY TRAINING SCHOOLS AIDED BY THE JOHN F. SLATER FUND, 1911 TO 1933 INCLUSIVE

Place of County Training Schools in Secondary Field 77

Several noteworthy characteristics are discernible from an analysis of the data presented. The fact that 399, or 65 per cent, of the County Training Schools now offer 4 years of secondary work indicates that Dr. Dillard's[3] early aspirations are materializing.[4] Furthermore, his plan to develop *rural* high schools has shown progress, since 57.6 per cent of these 4-year schools are located in rural localities.

No less important is the fact that 75 per cent of the 612 schools are located in the eight states having the largest Negro constituencies of approximate secondary school age.[5] Moreover, 77 per cent of the total high school population resides within these eight states. Of the 459 schools in these states, 73 per cent are found in the open country or villages and towns having less than 2,500 inhabitants. County Training Schools, therefore, are most numerous in states having the largest Negro populations, and are so located as to be of possible service to the majority of Negroes dwelling in rural communities.

Interpreting Table XIX more rigorously, it is seen that certain exceptions to the general trends indicated stand out. Arkansas, Mississippi and South Carolina are conspicuous in that they are the only states wherein less than 50 per cent of the Training Schools have developed into four-year high schools. Undoubtedly numerous factors contributed to this somewhat slower development. The County Training School movement, however, has been active in each of these states for 19 years or more.[6]

Florida, Kentucky and Tennessee differ from the other states in that the majority of schools aided by the Fund are in urban locations. This difference is, sometimes, the result of the evolution of small rural towns into urban centers,—undoubtedly an instrumental factor in giving the data an urban emphasis in Kentucky and Tennessee. It naturally holds true, in greater or lesser degree, for all states. Then, too, if transportation is provided, the rural secondary student suffers less from the standpoint of school location. Kentucky, in particular, is trans-

---

[3] General Agent and Later President of the Slater Fund, 1910-1931.
[4] See Chapter II, p. 35.
[5] Ranked in order: Georgia, North Carolina, Mississippi, Alabama, South Carolina, Texas, Louisiana and Virginia.
[6] Arkansas, 22 years; Mississippi, 21 years; South Carolina, 19 years. See Table XXIV, p. 84.

porting Negro secondary students in order to make schools more accessible.[7] In Florida, however, the transportation facilities are far less satisfactory. Furthermore, the schools in Florida in the category of County Training Schools are located principally in large urban localities which have not grown from rural origins during the life-time of the schools in question. While the data do not constitute incontrovertible evidence, they presage an urbanmindedness somewhere in the Training School movement in Florida.

To permit comparative analysis of the grouped County Training Schools projected against all public Negro Secondary schools, distinguishing percentages are given in Table XX.

TABLE XX

DISTRIBUTION OF COUNTY TRAINING SCHOOLS AND NON-SLATER-AIDED PUBLIC SECONDARY SCHOOLS AS TO LOCATION AND YEARS OF WORK OFFERED

Schools	Distribution by Years of Work Offered								Total
	1 Year		2 Years		3 Years		4 Years		
	Rural	Urban	Rural	Urban	Rural	Urban	Rural	Urban	
All Schools	340	62	373	89	271	61	388	419	2,003
County Training School Group:									
Number	25	6	72	22	67	21	230	169	612
Per Cent	7.4	9.7	19.3	24.7	24.4	34.4	59.3	40.3	30.5
Non-Slater-Aided Group:									
Number	315	56	301	67	204	40	158	250	1,391
Per Cent	92.6	90.3	80.7	75.3	75.6	65.6	40.7	59.7	69.5

It is at once apparent that 30.5 per cent of all public Negro secondary schools have been, at sometime, identified with the County Training School movement. An exceedingly persistent tendency is apparent as one surveys the percentages running from left to right. The non-training schools decidedly include the larger proportion of all rural and urban schools offering one, two, and three years of secondary work. It indicates that the very questionable endeavor of one and two teacher schools (mostly rural) to stretch their meagre educational assets to include the first and second grades of high

[7] In 1932-33 Slater aid was used to assist in transporting Negro secondary pupils from one county to another as follows: From Greenup County to Ashland, Boyd County; Hancock County to Hardinsburg in Breckinridge County; Knott County to Vicco in Perry County; Meade County to Hardinsburg in Breckinridge County; and from Powell County to Winchester in Clark County.

school is confined virtually to schools entirely subsidized by public funds. In the Training School group, the reverse tendency is shown and, is entirely to be expected because only the larger elementary schools are selected to be developed into Training Schools.

The comparison of percentages indicative of the distribution of four-year schools clearly emphasizes both the need for stimulative effort on behalf of the rural Negro educable and the dividends yielded by years of effort in his interest. So it is, and has been from the beginning, that the economically favored urban authorities have tended to gather for their constituencies a disproportionate share of the educational goods. And in the case of the Negro, the minority urbanites have profited at the expense of their rural fellowmen. In this respect, at least, the County Training Schools have wielded a counter-active influence for the facts show that the distribution of the schools is more equitably consistent with the distribution of the Negro population.

The Accredited Training Schools

Previously it was indicated in Table XX that 49.4 per cent of the 807 four-year public secondary schools for Negroes in the South are included in the group of schools considered in this investigation in the category of County Training Schools. Of the 399 four-year Training Schools aided by the Slater Fund 45.5 per cent, or 181, have been fully accredited by the responsible state authorities. In addition to these schools there are 31 Parish Training Schools in Louisiana which have been approved by the State Division of Negro Education on a slight lower basis than that which is customary for the accredited schools.

The total enrollment in accredited Training Schools aggregated 20,085 pupils in 1933. This was but 25 per cent of the total enrollment in all accredited public secondary schools for Negroes in the South.

The average enrollment per accredited County Training School is 116 pupils, as contrasted to 205 pupils per school in the non-training school group. This disparity is undoubtedly attributable to the fact that 80 of the accredited Training

Schools are located in rural places, and the remainder are found almost exclusively in the smaller urban communities. It is almost too obvious to mention that the smaller secondary schools in the United States are found, usually, in the open country, villages, towns and lesser cities. Negro secondary schools are no exception to this national tendency.

Since 1932 the Slater Fund has maintained a policy of withdrawing aid from schools that have attained the status of four-year accredited state high schools.

The Enrollments Compared

In Table XXI data are so arranged as to yield information concerning comparative enrollments.

TABLE XXI
ENROLLMENT IN COUNTY TRAINING SCHOOL GROUP AND NON-SLATER-AIDED PUBLIC SECONDARY SCHOOLS FOR NEGROES IN SEVENTEEN SOUTHERN STATES, 1932-33

Schools	Enrollment by Type of School								
	1-Year		2-Year		3-Year		4-Year		
	Rural	Urban	Rural	Urban	Rural	Urban	Rural	Urban	Total
All Schools	2,784	3,915	6,344	2,667	7,960	4,665	30,662	89,757	148,754
County Training School Group:									
Number	272	115	1,433	790	2,456	1,488	20,273	19,591	46,418
Per Cent	9.7	2.9	22.6	29.6	30.0	31.8	66.0	21.9	31.2
Non-Slater-Aided Group:									
Number	2,512	3,800	4,911	1,877	5,504	3,177	10,389	70166	102,336
Per Cent	90.3	97.1	77.4	70.4	60.0	68.2	34.0	78.1	68.8

Appendix D includes complete State-by-State compilations of facts pertaining to the number of schools, the enrollment and number of teachers in 1-year, 2-year, 3-year, and 4-year County Training Schools.

The fact that 46,418 secondary pupils were enrolled in schools included in the County Training School group indicates that this group served 31.2 per cent of all Negroes who were enrolled in public secondary schools in the South in 1933. The same tendency noted in reference to the distribution of the schools naturally recurs with reference to the enrollment. Relatively few students were enrolled in County Training Schools wherein only one or two years of secondary work was offered. The reverse holds true for the non-Training School group, wherein were enrolled 83.4 per cent of the 15,710 children found in these "lesser" high schools. The comparison of enrollments in four-year schools again emphasizes the fact that the activity of the County Training School movement is greatest in rural areas.

Comparative Facts Concerning Size of Schools

One of the most important factors indicative of comparative differences is *size* as determined by enrollment.[8] Table XXII presents data pertaining to the average enrollment per school as an index of size.

TABLE XXII
Size of Schools Included in the County Training School Group and the Non-Slater-Aided Public Secondary Schools for Negroes in the South

Schools	Average Enrollment Per School by Types							
	1-Year		2-Year		3-Year		4-Year	
	Rural	Urban	Rural	Urban	Rural	Urban	Rural	Urban
County Training School Group	15	19	20	36	37	71	89	128
Non-Slater-Aided Group	7	7.3	16	28	27	79	73	264
All Schools	8	8	17	30	30	76	79	214

If there existed any doubt about the size of public Negro secondary schools in the South, the facts constituting this table dispels it with finality. Comparing the two groups involved in the presentation, it is apparent that, with but two exceptions, the average enrollment per school in the Training School group is larger than the non-Slater-aided group. The exceptions are the three-year urban schools where the difference is relatively small, and the four-year urban non-training-school group of schools, where the difference is greater. If it is true, and competent investigators affirm it,[9] that the problems of secondary schools, in general, multiply as the size of their enrollments decrease, then those persons who administer the affairs of public secondary education should be made aware of the smallness of Negro high schools.

[8]Ferris, E. N., Guamnitz, W. H., and Brammell, P. R. *The Smaller Secondary Schools*, pp. 232-236.
[9]Gaumnitz, W. H. *The Smallness of America's Rural High Schools*, pp. 67-76.
Cyr, Frank W. (editor). *The Economical Enrichment of the Small Secondary-School Curriculum*, The Department of Rural Education of the National Education Association, Washington, D. C., 1934.

The Secondary Teachers in County Training Schools

Recapitulating the essential numerical facts pertaining to the teachers in public Negro secondary schools in the South, it should be recalled that 5,298 full time and 1,478 part time teachers constituted this group. Of this total, 33 per cent were in schools comprising the County Training School group and, as such, numbered 1,782 full time, and 422 part time teachers. Sixty-four per cent of the Training School secondary teachers are in the rural County Training Schools. This is not remarkable since 60 per cent of all such schools are in rural places. The fact, however, that only 53 per cent of the total number of pupils enrolled in County Training were found in the rural schools indicates that their pupil-teacher ratio was lower. Keeping these facts in mind, attention is called to Table XXIII, which includes data on the average number of teachers per school.

TABLE XXIII
THE AVERAGE NUMBER OF TEACHERS PER SCHOOL IN THE COUNTY TRAINING SCHOOL GROUP AND THE NON-SLATER-AIDED PUBLIC SECONDARY SCHOOLS FOR NEGROES IN THE SOUTH

Secondary Teachers	Average Number of Teachers per School by Type of School			
	1-Year	2-Year	3-Year	4-Year
County Training School Group:				
Full Time	.5	1.0	1.8	3.8
Part Time	.8	.9	.6	.6
Non-Slater-Aided Group:				
Full Time	.2	.6	1.2	6.9
Part Time	.9	.7	.6	.7
All Schools:				
Full Time	.3	.8	1.4	5.3
Part Time	.9	.8	.6	.7

The typical County Training School offering four years of secondary work is staffed with three full-time secondary teachers and two other teachers who serve in a part-time capacity. By comparison, the four-year non-Slater-aided school has a larger staff. The problem of providing an adequate secondary program is more acute in the Training School, since few teachers necessitate the extension of the services of the individual teacher over a greater number of subject fields.

The comparison of the average teaching staff in one, two,

and three-year schools reveals that the County Training Schools are better staffed, numerically, than other public secondary schools.

COUNTY TRAINING SCHOOLS AND PUBLIC SECONDARY EDUCATIONAL PROVISION FOR NEGROES

As a means of revealing the extensiveness of the County Training School movement, it was shown that the Slater Fund was actively interested in one or more schools in 352 counties in the South during 1933. In 205 counties the Training School was, indeed, *sine qua non*, since it offered the sole public secondary facilities available to the ambitious Negro student. Still thinking of the County Training School in this same sense, it is the purpose of this section to consider all the schools located in 15 states which have been at any time identified with this movement from 1911 to 1933. The 517 counties in which these schools are located include 56.7 per cent of all counties offering some public secondary education for Negroes in 1933. By analyzing the distribution of schools in each state, the results depicted in Table XXIV were obtained.

In so far as the presence in a county of at least one school offering public secondary work describes that county's educational provision, the data presented have significance. Schools providing public high school work for Negroes were found in 912 counties in the 15 states included in this phase of the investigation. In 293 counties, or 32.1 per cent of the total number, the only schools offering any public education whatever were County Training Schools. In 198 instances the school offered four years of secondary work. The Negro population 15 to 19 years of age in these counties aggregated 281,245 persons. That is, 28.5 per cent of all Negro persons included within this age range in 15 states lived in these counties. The secondary enrollment in these Training Schools was 21,681 pupils. Hence 7.8 per cent of the approximate Negro secondary population sought secondary educational opportunities in these schools. So it is seen that, although the presence of at least one high school in a county is an asset, a real problem exists in making the schools accessible to greater numbers. Some Training Schools possess dormitories, but these, in general, are too few

TABLE XXIV

Counties in Fifteen Southern States Wherein County Training Schools Provide the *Only* Public Secondary Work and Other Counties Wherein These Schools Offer the *Most Advanced* Public Secondary Work

State	Counties in State Offering Some Secondary Work		Negro Population 15-19 years of age	Counties Wherein County Training Schools Provide Only Secondary Work		Counties Wherein County Training Schools Provide Most Advanced Secondary Work		Total of B and C		Number of Years of Slater Aid
	No.		A	No.	Per cent of "A" living in these Counties B	No.	Per cent of "A" living in these Counties C	Number of Counties	Per Cent D	
Arkansas	42		47,732	19	53.4	4	18.3	23	71.7	22
Mississippi	66		98,939	27	40.4	9	24.5	36	64.9	21
Virginia	72		67,759	49	55.1	3	4.1	52	59.2	20
Louisiana	46		68,479	26	48.3	5	5.7	31	54.0	22
Alabama	57		105,409	21	30.2	12	22.3	33	52.5	20
Florida	38		37,275	16	38.5	3	9.9	19	48.4	14
South Carolina	46		106,429	5	11.3	21	36.6	26	47.9	19
Kentucky	64		19,140	34	39.0	1	2.2	35	41.2	19
Georgia	118		123,000	36	29.3	11	10.9	47	40.2	20
Tennessee	55		49,420	25	36.3	1	1.3	26	37.6	18
North Carolina	88		114,555	27	18.2	11	12.3	38	30.5	19
Texas	130		91,335	2	1.9	19	21.4	21	23.3	19
Oklahoma	38		17,205	3	9.0	3	8.3	6	17.3	13
Missouri	32		16,284	2	3.7	1	1.0	3	4.7	3
Maryland	20		24,412	1	3.6			1	3.6	11
Total	912		987,373	293	28.5	104	15.7	397	44.2	

Note: The states are listed in the rank order of the percentages shown in column "D."

Place of County Training Schools in Secondary Field 85

to be of any considerable advantage to the vast numbers who live beyond the radius of daily attendance.

Besides the three hundred ninety-three counties discussed above there were 104 other counties wherein the most advanced public secondary facilities[10] were provided only by the County Training Schools. In 89 of the 104 counties, these schools offered a four-year program of studies. The number of pupils enrolled in the secondary grades of Training Schools in the 104 counties was 10,382. Residing within the counties were approximately 155,-500 Negroes, constituting 15.7 per cent of the total 15 to 19 years age group found in 15 Southern states. It can be seen from Table XXIV that, of the 987,373 Negroes of high school age who lived in counties providing some public secondary work in 1933, 44.2 per cent resided in counties wherein County Training Schools offered the *only*, or the *most advanced*, high school education provided at public expense.

Great variability characterizes the percentages indicative of the extent to which Negroes in the several states sought their only, or most advanced, public high school education in County Training Schools. Arkansas with 71.7 per cent presented one extreme and Maryland, with 3.6 per cent, the other. In general those states having the greater Negro population seem to depend most upon the secondary function discharged through the Training Schools. The conspicuous exceptions to this tendency are Arkansas, Florida and Kentucky, with relatively small Negro populations and high percentages of dependency upon County Training Schools; and North Carolina and Texas, with large Negro populations and lesser dependency upon these schools. Table XXV presents data so arranged as to aid in considering the atypical cases just mentioned.

Arkansas

Arkansas enrolled but 6.9 per cent of its total estimated Negro secondary population in 1933, while seven states with substantially larger Negro population enrolled larger percentages. It has been shown that this state had 57.9 per cent of its Negro population living in counties offering *less* than four years of secondary work.[11] This is a higher percentage than any other

[10] The highest grade or year of secondary work offered.
[11] See Table XVII, p. 72.

TABLE XXV

Relation of Negro Population, 15 to 19 Years of Age, in Fifteen Southern States to (a) Per Cent Enrolled in Public Secondary Schools for Negroes; (b) Per Cent Living in Counties Wherein County Training Schools Provide the Only, or Most Advanced, Secondary Work†

State	Negro Population 15 to 19 Years of Age			
	Total Number in State	Per cent Enrolled in Public Secondary Schools	No. in Counties Providing Some Secondary Work (A)	Per cent of (A) in Counties Where Training Schools Provide Only, or Most Advanced, Secondary Work
Missouri	17,735	27.7	16,284	4.7
Oklahoma	18,811	31.3	17,205	17.3
Kentucky	20,762	24.6	19,140	41.2*
Maryland	25,417	20.7	24,412	3.6
Florida	43,355	12.0*	37,275	48.4*
Tennessee	51,835	16.7	49,420	37.6
Arkansas	52,545	6.9*	47,732	71.7*
Virginia	73,443	15.6	67,759	59.2
Louisiana	81,293	9.2	68,479	54.0
Texas	92,696	24.4*	91,335	23.3*
South Carolina	106,429	9.9	106,429	47.9
Alabama	109,216	8.0	105,409	52.5
Mississippi	114,893	5.2	98,939	64.9
North Carolina	115,166	20.0*	114,555	30.5*
Georgia	134,216	7.7	123,000	40.2
Total	1,057,812	13.1	987,373	44.2

†Compiled from data included in Tables X and XXIV.
*Seem to be exceptions when the percentages are considered in relation to the Negro populations of the states.

Southern state yielded. Table XVII also shows that the average number of Negroes 15 to 19 years of age per county was 1,051 which figure is exceeded by the figures for six other states. Despite the fact that 80 per cent of the Negro population is rural, there were but five four-year public secondary schools located in non-urban centers. Of the 36 schools identified at some time as County Training Schools, ten offer four-year secondary programs, and only two of these are located in rural communities. The facts indicate a most unfavorable situation as far as Negro secondary educables are concerned.

Several factors, the relative importance of which cannot be accurately estimated, could be responsible. The area of counties would seem important. Other states, however, have equally large counties and seem to provide more adequately for Negro secondary pupils. Transportation of pupils is another consideration. It appears that few Negro students are transported.[12] This aggravates the rural student's predicament. State control through supervision and high school classification is another conditioning aspect. The facts indicate that much local autonomy is effective. The State authorities classify secondary schools only at the request or invitation of the local school authorities. Provision is made for accrediting schools as 6-3, 6-4, 6-6, 6-3-3, 8-3, 8-2, and 8-4 organizations, thereby allowing for much variation.

The status of the county superintendency is decidedly problematical, with that office being, at least temporarily, abolished. In addition, the entire program of instruction, and consequently, of organization, is undergoing a change. These recent changes, while important, have hardly been responsible for what seems to be a cumulative condition in Negro secondary education.

The County Training School movement has been active in Arkansas for 22 years. An average of 8.5 years aid to a county characterizes the distribution for all counties assisted since 1911. The fact that 71.7 per cent of the Negroes of high school age who were in counties providing some secondary work in 1933, resided in counties wherein County Training Schools offered most of that which constituted public secondary education—is testimony to the Training School's importance to the minority race. On the other hand, the fact that only ten Training Schools offered four years of secondary work, and only two of these were in rural localities, indicates a development not entirely consistent with comparative developmental tendencies evidenced in other states.

Florida

Only four Southern states have fewer Negroes 15 to 19 years of age than Florida. Twelve per cent of those included in this age

[12]Figures which differentiate between transportation expenditures for Negro and white children are available for 1932. During this year the sums expended for Negro and white children were $5,844 and $592,660 respectively. The population ratio of Negroes to whites in this state is 1 to 3.9.
Phipps, W. E. *Biennial Report of the State Commissioner of Education.* State of Arkansas, 1932-33; 1933-34, pp. 155-160.

group in the state were enrolled in the public secondary schools. Of the total approximate Negro secondary population in Florida 24.4 per cent[13] lived in counties providing less than four years of public high school work in 1933. At the same time it should be noted that 48.4 per cent of the state's total potential high school population resided in counties wherein schools included in the category of County Training Schools provided most of the public secondary facilities available for Negroes.

In this state the county is primarily the administrative unit. Counties in Florida are relatively large in area, as compared with many counties in the Southern states, and the average number of potential Negro secondary students aggregates 647 persons per county. With the exception of those counties wherein are found the larger cities the Negro population is generally scattered in rural areas or grouped around rural communities, many of which are so small as to question the expediency of establishing high schools. While a small amount of transportation is provided for Negro secondary students, the facilities are far from adequate.[14] With existing public secondary schools so predominantly urban, the rural Negro must either provide much of his own transportation, or arrange to board near the school. Few states are faced with a more difficult Negro educational problem so inextricably related to the inter- and intracounty transportation problem. In addition, there are counties and communities so educationally retarded in general that schools for both races are equally inadequate. This, of course, is true of other counties in other states of the South. Unfortunately for Negroes, historical evidence indicates that the schools for whites usually attain a definite degree of development before the educational needs of the less privileged race will receive much consideration.

Seventeen out of twenty-three Florida schools listed as County Training Schools are in urban locations, although 52 per cent of the Negro population is rural. Fourteen of these offer four years of high school work, and all are located in the larger towns and cities. The evidence indicates that they represent a departure from the early policy of the Slater Fund

[13]See Table XVII, p. 72.
[14]Caliver, Ambrose. *Secondary Education for Negroes*, p. 22.

for stimulating the development of secondary schools which would be available and adapted to the needs of a large rural Negro constituency.

North Carolina.

In comparison with other Southern states North Carolina has a Negro population 15 to 19 years of age exceeded only by Georgia. Contrasted with all states possessing more than 40,000 Negroes included in this age range, North Carolina is exceeded only by Texas in the percentage of potential high school population that was enrolled in the state's secondary schools in 1933. Using the same 11 states as a basis for comparison, Texas is the only state appearing to be less dependent upon County Training Schools than North Carolina. Table XVII shows that only 2.7 per cent of the Negro secondary population of North Carolina resided in counties offering less than four years of high school work.

Of the one hundred counties in North Carolina, nineteen have Negro populations too small[15] to justify a four-year accredited high school. Thirteen have sufficient population, but have not yet developed an accredited school.

Sixty-four of the 99 public accredited secondary schools have received aid from the Slater Fund as County Training Schools. The County Training School movement has been actively supported in North Carolina for nineteen years.

Texas

It is seen from Table XXV that Texas enrolled 24.4 per cent of the Negro population 15 to 19 years of age in the State in public secondary schools in 1933. Of this age group, 11.9 per cent resided in counties offering less than four years of public high school work.

It should be stated that Texas has 254 counties, 117 of which have fewer than fifty Negro inhabitants 15 to 19 years of age. Most of the 117 counties are in the Western and Southern parts of the State, where the counties are relatively large in area. The bulk of the Negro population is concentrated in the North-

[15] Approximately sixty in the 15-19 age-group. This is based upon figures submitted by a representative of the Division of Negro Education in North Carolina.

eastern part of Texas, where the counties are relatively small. Another factor of importance in interpreting the county-by-county analyses concerns the large number of independent districts in the state. Distributed among 80 counties are 178 independent districts embracing populations of less than 2,500 persons. No one knows the exact degree of cooperation which characterizes these districts and the neighboring county districts.

The County Training School movement was initiated in Texas nineteen years ago. The schools are highly regarded by the State educational authorities and the local constituencies.[16]

The Other States.

Tennessee, Virginia, Louisiana, South Carolina, Alabama, Mississippi and Georgia are the remaining states having the larger Negro secondary populations. As a group they tend to rely greatly upon the County Training Schools to provide secondary facilities for Negro students. Furthermore, by studying Table XVI again it is seen that with the possible exception of Virginia, each state possessed a considerable number of counties providing little or no high school facilities. These states, as a group, enroll relatively low percentages of their potential Negro secondary population. These states have many factors peculiar to their counties and the distributions of Negro population which necessitate careful study before any large program for development of secondary schools should be attempted. A case in point is South Carolina which, as compared with other Southern states, has relatively large counties with heavy Negro population and no transportation facilities to speak of.[17] Georgia, with many small counties which possess Negro population ranging from none to many thousands, can hope to do little without transportation and consolidation. To be more specific, there are thirty counties in this state wherein it will be most difficult to develop high school work without some system of transportation. Merely by mentioning these few conditioning factors some conception of the difficulties in developing high schools can be sensed. *It*

---

[16] Davis, W. R. *The Development and Present Status of Negro Education in East Texas*, pp. 73-75.
[17] Caliver, Ambrose, op. cit., p. 22.

is in these states that outside agencies should concentrate their efforts to be of assistance in bettering educational conditions for Negroes.

Missouri, Oklahoma, Kentucky and Maryland, in comparison with the other Southern states have fewer potential Negro secondary students 15 to 19 years of age. As a group they enroll the higher percentages of this Negro population in high schools. They draw less heavily upon the Training Schools for the secondary facilities they offer. Kentucky, however, has 35 counties wherein schools which are now or were formerly identified with the Training School movement still provide all that is offered in high school work for the Negro inhabitants. Pursuing the principle of furnishing assistance upon the basis of greatest need, these states, as a group, need much less aid than the group of states previously mentioned.

A word of caution might be inserted at this point. Throughout this discussion there have been frequent comparisons drawn within and between the several states of the South. It must be remembered that such comparisons are within a given section of the United States, and that there is always the national standard to be consulted for broader interpretation. Beyond this national limit is always the opportunity to judge in terms of the best standards of achievement the world can furnish.

STATE RECOGNITION OF COUNTY TRAINING SCHOOLS

The preceeding pages of this presentation have been concerned largely with factual data of statistical and purely historical nature. One source of information remains to be studied, that is, the reactions of state educational authorities as exemplified in official publications.

Legal Status

A review of legislation and the school laws of the several states wherein County Training Schools for Negroes are found revealed only one case of special legislation referring to these schools. In revising and codifying the school laws of North Carolina in 1923 a provision was included authorizing county boards of education to establish one county training school for not less than an eight-month term for either race, in which elementary and high school subjects, agriculture, home economics, special industrial subjects, and methods of teaching were to be taught.[18] Evidently the powers and authority given to county and local boards to establish elementary and high schools in the several states served as an adequate legal basis for the establishment of these schools.[19] This does not seem unusual in view of the fact that, from the beginning, Slater aid to these schools was granted only if the school property belonged to the state, county, or district, and was part of the public school system. In addition to this requirement the school was to be developed into a high school as soon as possible.

Statements of State Authorities

From time to time state educational authorities have given official recognition of the value and place of these schools in the field of public Negro education. Included in the annual report for 1928-1929 of T. H. Harris, the State Superintendent of Public Education of Louisiana, was the following comment:

"Since 1916 Louisiana has drawn from the Slater Fund freely for aid to stimulate and encourage the establishment and operation of Parish Training Schools . . . for Negroes.

"The welfare and development of training schools have claimed attention of local school officials and a large proportion of the time of the Division of Negro Education."[20]

An earlier report includes a statement referring to the number and calibre of these schools.

"There are 21 parish training schools which represent the best type of Negro schools in the State and which are rendering valuable assistance in training teachers for Negro school work."[21]

Under the heading, "Rural Secondary Education" the annual report of the Department of Education of Alabama for 1931 presents a report of the County Training School movement in that state. It outlines Dr. Dillard's early proposal to grant financial aid to any county which would establish such a school:

---

[18] Brooks, E. C. *The Public School Law of North Carolina.* Codification of 1923. State Department of Education, Section 41, 1923, p. 14.
[19] This statement was confirmed through special communication with the State Agents for Negro Education in fifteen Southern states.
[20] Harris, T. H. *Eightieth Annual Report of the State Superintendent of Public Education of Louisiana.* For the Session, 1928-1929, p. 70.
[21] Harris, T. H. *Sixty-seventh Annual Report of the State Superintendent of Public Instruction of Louisiana.* For the Session, 1925-1926, p. 42.

"The idea met with popular response throughout the South, and for the last 16 years the John F. Slater Fund has been cooperating liberally toward the stimulation of this particular phase of the program for public education for Negroes . . . . Out of this new venture came the type of secondary rural school known as the 'county training school,' the first of which was established at Cottage Grove, in Coosa County, in 1915. By the close of the year 1930-1931, 40 such schools had been built in Alabama. The teacher-training feature, however, was practiced in a limited way by only a few schools in this State."[22]

Dr. Nolen M. Irby, Supervisor of Negro Education in Arkansas, reports that during the school year of 1911-1912 the trustees of the Slater Fund aided in establishing four "County Training Schools," one of which was at Hope.

"It was established under the principalship of Henry C. Yerger, who is still serving in that same capacity. This training school, recently re-named by action of the local board of education, 'The Henry C. Yerger High School' has the distinction of being the oldest county training school in the United States . . . At present little teaching training activities are attemped, but the industrial training is still emphasized. Many have become standard high schools but still wish to be known as county training schools."[23]

Texas was one of the first states officially to recognize the utility of these schools in the field of Negro education.[24] A recent bulletin on Negro Education devoted a special section to consideration of the Training Schools. The following quotation indicates something of the nature and activities of these schools:

"A county training school, sponsored by the Slater Fund cooperating with public school authorities, is primarily a Negro high school. Texas had thirty-two of these schools in 1930-31. . . . . An attempt has been made, and to a degree successfully, so to modify and revise the course of study in these schools as to make them in fact, as well as in name, rural industrial high schools, meeting the needs of the rural communities in which they are located. In all the training schools some form of vocational work is offered; in a number of them courses in home economics, agriculture and farm shop work are available."[25]

---

[22] Harman, A. F. *Annual Report of the State Department of Education of Alabama.* For year ending June, 1931, pp. 80-84.
Feagin, W. F. *Annual Report of the Department of Education of the State of Alabama.* For the Scholastic Year ending September 30, 1916, pp. 76-77.
[23] Hirst, O. M. *Biennial Report of the State Commissioner of Education, Arkansas.* 1930-32, p. 57-58.
[24] Marrs, C. M. N. *The Twenty-second Biennial Report of the State Department of Education of Texas.* For the Biennium, 1920-22, p. 136.
The Twenty-fourth Biennial Report of the State Department of Education of Texas. For the Biennium, 1924-26, pp. 165-166.
[25] Marrs, S. M. N., Bludworth, G. T., and Taylor, D. B. *Negro Education in Texas.* Bulletin No. 294, 1931, State Department of Education, pp. 7-8.

W. R. Davis, in a recent study of the development of Negro Education in East Texas, finds that the County Training School movement is likely to exert an important influence on Negro education in the State.

"These schools are examples of the best there is in Negro education at the present time, and may serve as models to other Negro educational institutions . . . . That these schools are likely to exert an important influence on Negro education in Texas is seen in the recent growth of the County Training School movement . . . . While the number of County Training Schools in East Texas is far from adequate to meet the needs of Negro high school education in this section, these schools serve as a model to pattern after in the further development of Negro high schools. The vocational emphasis in the curricula of these schools not only makes them serviceable to the Negro population, but brings them into favor with the white people. Of the 32 schools of the State all but one have vocational work for boys and every one has a department of home economics."[26]

G. T. Bludworth stated in a paper read at Prairie View, March 18, 1932, that, " . . . a County Training School in a county . . . stimulates the entire Negro population educationally and has *some* effect on the white population."[27]

In much the same manner Georgia,[28] Kentucky,[29] South Carolina,[30] Mississippi,[31] North Carolina,[32] Tennessee,[33] and Virginia,[34] have recognized the worthiness of this particular development in the field of public secondary education for Negroes in the Southern states.

---

[26] Davis, W. R. *The Development and Present Status of Negro Education in East Texas,* p. 211.

[27] *Ibid.,* p. 215.

[28] Brittain, M. L. *Forty-fourth Annual Report of the Department of Education of the State of Georgia.* For the year ending December 15, 1915, p. 41.
Duggan, Mell. L. *Sixty-first Report of the Department of Education of the State of Georgia.* For the Biennium ending June 30, 1932, pp. 34-38.

[29] Colvin, G. *Report of the Superintendent of Public Instruction of Kentucky.* For the two years ending June 30, 1921, pp. 38-39; also the *Report* for the Biennium ending June 30, 1931, p. 155.

[30] Hope, James H. *Sixty-fifth Annual Report of the State Superintendent of Education of the State of South Carolina.* For the school session 1932-1933, pp. 30-31.

[31] Bond, W. F. *Biennial Report of the State Superintendent of Public Education of Mississippi.* For the Scholastic years 1921-23, pp. 74-79; also, Biennial Report, etc. For the Scholastic years 1923-25, pp. 19-21.

[32] Allen, A. T. *Biennial Report of the Superintendent of Public Instruction of North Carolina.* For the Scholastic years 1928-1929, and 1929-1930, p. 50.

[33] Sherrill, S. W. *Biennial Report of the State Superintendent of Public Instruction of Tennessee.* For the Scholastic years ending June 30, 1917-18, p. 15.
Brown, J. B. *Annual Report of the State Superintendent of Public Instruction of Tennessee.* For the Scholastic year ending June 30, 1922, pp. 272-276.

[34] Stearns, R. C. *Annual Report of the Superintendent of Public Instruction of Virginia.* School year, 1917-1918, pp. 52-53.
Hart, Harris, *Annual Report of the Superintendent of Public Instruction of Virginia.* School year, 1923-1924, p. 38.
Hall, Sidney B. *Annual Report of the Superintendent of Public Instruction of Virginia.* School year, 1931-1932, p. 70.

Chapter V

SUMMARY AND INTERPRETATION

THE DEVELOPMENT OF COUNTY TRAINING SCHOOLS FOR NEGROES[1]

IN 1911, the John F. Slater Fund, through its administrative personnel, became interested in stimulating the development of publicly supported secondary schools for the Negroes of the South. In the light of available documentary evidence it seems that there were but sixty-four urban and few rural public secondary schools for this minority race at that time. Intent upon alleviating the educational ills of the race at their very source, the Fund, in cooperation with public officials, sponsored the development of schools adapted to the needs of rural Negroes. In short, the purpose of these "County Training Schools" was to offer a more advanced public education based upon a necessary adaptation to the demands of rural life and the training of teachers for rural schools within the county.

Four such schools located in Arkansas, Louisiana and Mississippi initiated the movement. Four years later, in 1915, twenty-nine schools in ten states had been established. The venture then gathered momentum and by 1920 had embraced 142 counties in fourteen states. The determined expansion of the movement reached its peak in 1931 when County Training Schools in 390 counties in fifteen states were assisted. There is every reason to believe that the development would have continued to spread had it not been for the drastic financial retrenchments precipitated by the economic instability of the current depression era. In 1933 three hundred fifty-six schools located in fourteen states were being aided as County Training Schools.

The significant growth of County Training Schools was not accidental. Behind it was, perhaps, the most noteworthy cooperative effort to be found in the annals of American public education. The evidence clearly reveals that at various times the following groups definitely participated in the move-

[1] See Chapters II and IV for detailed treatment of the findings summarized in this section.

ment: The General Education Board, The Julius Rosenwald Fund, The Carnegie Corporation, and The Peabody Fund. And to these must be added the assistance lent these schools by Smith-Hughes funds, support from state, county, and local tax funds and the innumerable contributions from individuals of both races.

The policies effective in the allocation of Slater aid were designed to strengthen the sense of responsibility of public authorities for providing more advanced educational facilities for Negroes in rural areas, and to raise the standards as rapidly as possible. The data indicate that in 517 counties in fifteen states the public school officials lent their aid to this movement in Negro secondary education. These school authorities co-operated with the Fund in the establishment and maintenance of 612 schools during the years 1911 to 1933. In the allocation of monies distributed through the Slater Fund, appropriations were dependent upon like or larger sums being raised for the specific purpose from public sources. The data show that the ratio of public monies paid for salaries in County Training Schools to sums disbursed through the Slater Fund for the same purpose grew from one and a half to one in 1912, to almost eighteen to one in 1930. The evidence justifies the conclusion that public support was stimulated to a marked degree. It is of paramount significance that, since these schools were to be *public* schools, their main development has been effected through public school funds.

Another condition stipulated that the teaching had to extend through the eighth grade with the intention of adding higher grades as soon as possible. The evidence shows that 399 of the 612 schools offered four years of secondary work and that 181 of these were fully accredited. Quite apparently these County Training Schools have shown a decided tendency to develop into acceptable public secondary schools.

The effort to offer public secondary facilities to the *rural* student has been carried out with a high degree of consistency. Eighty per cent of the County Training Schools offering one year, seventy-six per cent of those offering two years, seventy-six per cent of those offering three years, and fifty-seven per cent of those schools offering a full four-year secondary course, are located in the open country or in small rural communities. These figures undoubtedly would have been somewhat greater had it been possible to make due allowance for those localities which have attained urban status since the schools were first established. The evidence, however, does not indicate that the effort in this direction has been uniformly successful in all states.

The name County Training School connotes an educational function which was of utmost significance in the earlier years of the movement. In setting as a goal the training of teachers for rural elementary schools, those in charge were striking with unerring direction at what was a most vulnerable spot in the Negro educational field. Completely satisfactory objective data concerning both the qualitative and quantitative importance of the effort in this direction are unavailable for all states.

Louisiana, probably more than any other state, capitalized and encouraged the Training School movement for its teacher-training possibilities from the beginning. This state is the only one in the South, today, still encouraging this work in the Training Schools. Experienced teachers, called "teacher-trainers," are employed; the work is carefully supervised by members of the Division of Negro Education in the State Department of Education; and State Teacher's certificates are issued to graduates of these schools. In the other states this work was always more informal in nature. Today this function of the County Training School is no longer of primary importance.

Some of these County Training Schools, located in urban places, have become high schools and have lost their early identities as schools adapted to the needs of rural Negro children. These tend to conform to the pattern of the conventional American high school. The majority, however, represent an unusual type of consolidated school, offering the regular high school subjects and, in addition, a variety of courses and community services adapted to the needs of the agrarian Negro.

THE PRESENT STATUS OF PUBLIC SECONDARY EDUCATION FOR NEGROES[2]

There were 1,081,600 Negroes between 15 and 19 years of age in the District of Columbia and the seventeen Southern states

[2] See Chapter III for detailed treatment of the findings summarized in this section.

maintaining separate schools for the races in 1933. They are the children of a minority race and no argument consistent with the educational mores of the democratic society of which they are a part, can deny that they deserve as equitable a quantitative and qualitative share of the educational goods as is provided the majority race. This is particularly true in the field of public secondary education. An aim of this study was to discover a more complete and reliable body of data relative to this field than had been available heretofore. There follows a summary and interpretation of the more important findings relative to status:

Number of Schools

1. There were 2,003 public schools in the South offering one to four years of secondary work to Negroes in 1933. Of this number, 631 were found in urban centers possessing 2,500 or more inhabitants.
2. These schools, when classified according to the number of years of work offered, are distributed in the following manner:
    a. Of the rural schools, 340 offer one year, 373 offer 2 years, 271 offer 3 years and 388 offer 4 years of secondary work.
    b. Of the urban schools, 62 offer one year, 89 offer 2 years, 61 offer 3 years, and 419 offer 4 years of secondary work.

While 69 per cent of all public Negro secondary schools included in this study are located in rural areas wherein is found 67.4 per cent of the total Negro population, the fact remains that the urban population is greatly favored in the distribution of those educational opportunities which are provided for Negroes. The fact that 84.6 per cent of all one year, 80.7 per cent of all 2-year, and 81.6 per cent of all 3-year, schools were in rural localities, indicates that 67.4 per cent of the total Negro population is provided with somewhat more than a fair share of the lesser public secondary schools. This 67.4 per cent of the population is provided with but 48.1 per cent of the four-year schools while the urban minority of the Negro race in the South has 51.9 per cent of the schools offering four years of secondary work.

The Accredited Public Secondary Schools for Negroes

There were 807 four-year public Negro secondary schools in the South in 1933 and 367 had been fully accredited by State Departments of Education. Forty-seven of this accredited group have also been

Summary and Interpretation

placed upon the accredited list of the regional accrediting agencies functioning in these states. The fact that 224 of the accredited schools are located in urban communities indicates a further unfavorable distribution of secondary educational opportunities for the rural dweller.

Some indication of the variability in methods and standards for accrediting is shown by the numerical distribution of accredited schools among the several states. Four states—Florida, Louisiana, Mississippi and South Carolina—reported only 16 fully accredited 4-year public secondary schools for Negroes in 1933. All are located in large urban centers. On the other hand, North Carolina and Virginia had a total of 127 accredited schools which were almost equally divided as to urban-rural distribution. This quantitative disparity is hardly a reliable index for judging the qualitative merits of a school as is implied in accrediting. Some unaccredited schools in Louisiana and South Carolina would be fully accredited in certain other states.

By and large the data reflect a tendency to accredit the larger urban public Negro secondary schools.

The Public Negro Secondary School Enrollment

1. There were 148,754 pupils enrolled in 2,003 public Negro secondary schools in the South in 1933.
2. The rural schools enrolled 47,750 pupils, while 101,004 students were included in the urban schools.

Although there were 1,372 rural secondary schools, they enrolled only 32 per cent of the total secondary enrollment. On the other hand 631 urban schools enrolled 68 per cent of the secondary enrollment.

3. The one-year schools enrolled 6,699 pupils; the 2-year schools, 9,011; the 3-year schools, 12,625, and 120,319 were included in the 4-year schools.
4. Of the 148,754 pupils enrolled, 38.8 per cent were in the first year, 27.2 per cent in the second, 19.3 per cent in the third, and 14.7 per cent were found in the last year. These percentages roughly measure the quota expected to survive from one year to the next.
5. 53.3 per cent of all public secondary school Negro students were enrolled in fully accredited 4-year schools.

Caliver found that only 8.6 per cent of those who enroll in Negro secondary schools graduate and that 35.0 per cent of these continue their education in some college or university. Recent studies of Negro higher education have urged greater selectivity in admissions to eliminate, at the outset, many who will fail later. Generally speaking, we might expect about 2,700 graduates from accredited schools to matriculate at some higher institution. It so happens that over 9,000 students were admitted to freshmen classes in 118 public and private Negro colleges and universities in September, 1933. After making liberal allowances for pupils from private and public schools in the non-Southern states, it is obvious that the supply of properly prepared graduates from 4-year accredited secondary schools cannot meet the student-demands of the present number of Negro higher institutions to make possible selective admissions except for a very few colleges.

6. Of the total Negro population in the South ranging from 15 to 19 years of age, 13.7 per cent were enrolled in public secondary schools. Making allowance for private school and elementary enrollment absorption it can conservatively be stated that 930,000 Negroes of potential secondary school age were not enrolled in schools.

Great variability exists among the states with respect to the percentage of the Negro secondary population enrolled in public high schools. West Virginia, Oklahoma, Delaware, Missouri, Kentucky, Texas, Maryland and North Carolina enrolled 20 per cent or more while South Carolina, Louisiana, Alabama, Georgia, Arkansas and Mississippi enrolled less than 10 per cent of the 15 to 19 years age group within their respective confines.

There is a marked tendency among the states for their percentages enrolled in public secondary schools to decrease as the potential secondary population increases.

The Size of Negro Secondary Schools

Public secondary schools for Negroes are small no matter where they are found. Consider the following facts:
1. Only 18 out of 1,372 rural schools enrolled more than 200 pupils, while 97 per cent enrolled less than 151 students.
2. Seventy out of 631 urban secondary schools enrolled more than 300 pupils, while 73.1 per cent enrolled less than 151 students.
3. The average enrollment per school follows:
    a. Rural schools—1-year, 8; 2-year, 17; 3-year, 30; and 4-year, 79 pupils.
    b. Urban schools—1-year, 8; 2-year, 30; 3-year, 76; and 4-year, 214 pupils.

Summary and Interpretation

Unless consolidation, with transportation or board facilities, is practiced to a far greater extent than indicated at present these small schools will remain and may even increase. What ever may be the problems inherent in small secondary schools, they also are the problems of practically all public secondary schools for Negroes. In the case of the latter, however, they are far more acute due to the limitations imposed upon a minority group, for whom are reserved the less desirable aspects of a dual system of education.

The Instructional Staff

1. There were 6,776 teachers employed in public secondary schools for Negroes in the Southern states in 1933. Of this number 5,298 were full-time secondary teachers and the remainder divided their services between the elementary and secondary grades.
2. A total of 3,575 teachers were employed in rural schools, 2,423 of whom devoted full time to the secondary subjects.
3. The more advanced the secondary work offered in a school the greater the chances are that full time teachers are employed while the reverse is true for part-time teachers.
4. The secondary work in the average one-year school commands the services of one part-time teacher; the two-year school employs either two part-time teachers or one full-time teacher and less than half of the part-time teacher's service; the three-year school uses one full-time teacher and the major portion of a part-time teacher's service, while the average four-year school employs five full-time teachers and one part-time teacher. In the four-year school the principal may be considered as a full-time secondary teacher. The same is, more often than not, true for the "Smith-Hughes" teacher.

General

1. Three noteworthy relationships were discovered in studying the facts pertaining to public Negro secondary schools. They are the points of concentration around which the majority of the problems of the small secondary school gravitate. While significant for all public secondary schools, they are particularly important for the *rural* schools which constituted more than two-thirds of the total provided for Negroes. Consider the following:
   a. 69 per cent of all Negro secondary schools were rural.
   b. 32 per cent of the total secondary enrollment was rural.
   c. 53 per cent of all secondary teachers were found in rural schools.

Therefore, educators interested in Negro rural secondary schools must contend with the problems inherently relative to:

first, a low pupil-teacher ratio; second, a low pupil-per-school ratio; and third, a low teacher-per-school ratio.

2. Another finding well worthy of particular mention, concerns the disproportionate number of the "lesser" public Negro secondary schools. 43 per cent of all schools included in this investigation offer two years or less of *secondary* work. Furthermore, it is probable that there are more of the one-year type which for one reason or another were not reported by the different county and state officials. Hence, the importance of calling attention to them.

Over 80 per cent of all such schools are located either in the open country or in small rural communities. The average school in this category does not command the service of one full-time secondary teacher and enrolls only 8 to 17 secondary pupils. The data indicate that these schools are largely one- and two-teacher rural elementary schools struggling to cater to a growing demand from the Negroes themselves for public secondary education. Rural Negro elementary schools, as a group, represent much that is least desirable in the profession of education as it is practiced today. Their offering of *elementary* education is disproportionately weak in view of the best practice. In attempting to expand this offering to include the secondary grades it is almost inevitable that the educational outcomes will be further diluted. Such Negro *secondary* schools should be kept to the lowest possible number.

Organization of Public Secondary Schools for Negroes

1. Fifty-eight per cent of the total Negro population of potential secondary age in the South resides in Georgia, Louisiana, Maryland, North Carolina, South Carolina, Texas and Virginia. With the exception of six city systems, all Negro schools within these states had eleven-grade school systems with the conventional four-year high school composed of grades eight through eleven in 1933. The only *reorganized* (junior-senior high school modification) schools for Negroes found in these states were in four large city systems.
2. In the ten remaining states included in this study, twelve-grade systems prevail. Mississippi, Missouri, Oklahoma, Tennessee and Kentucky are almost uniformly committed to the conventional 8-4 system for Negro schools with grades nine through twelve constituting the secondary division. Ten city systems, however, in these states reported 6-3-3 or 6-6 organizations.

Alabama, Delaware, Florida and West Virginia have attempted to reorganize practically all Negro schools in so far as the last six years constitute the secondary grades. Arkansas, generally speaking, reported a majority of schools as possessing the 6-year elementary organization.

3. About 71,000 Negro students were enrolled in the last *six* grades of school systems employing reorganizations involving some modification of the 6-year secondary school scheme.

With the exception of eighteen or twenty city systems wherein separate 3-year junior and senior high schools are maintained, most of the reorganized schools for Negroes found in the South are in reality attempts to operate 6-year high schools. The extent to which actual reorganized procedures have been effected varies greatly. Many of these schools have failed to incorporate supposedly desirable features of reorganization through which greater educational efficiency should result. The reorganized schools have, however, generally adopted a somewhat more comprehensive and flexible organization than that which characterizes many of the more conventionally organized schools. The vast majority of Negroes must seek secondary educational opportunities in schools which, as yet, have not been reorganized.

PUBLIC SECONDARY EDUCATIONAL PROVISION FOR NEGROES IN THE SOUTH BY COUNTIES[3]

It is of great importance to children and their parents that a school of a given type should be located either in their immediate community or within the larger division for local government and school administration within which they live. In the South this larger division is the county for all states except Louisiana, where it is called *parish*. The extent to which public Negro secondary schools are provided in the counties in the 17 Southern states is summarized as follows:

Counties Having Little or No Negro Population

There are 1,501 counties in these states. Of this number, 373 had a Negro population, 15 to 19 years of age, of less than 50 persons in 1930. A total of 4,701 individuals within this age group resided in these counties and the mean number per county was 12.5 persons. Ninety per cent of these counties are found in Arkansas, Kentucky, Missouri, Oklahoma, Tennessee, Texas and West Virginia.

[3] See Chapter III for detailed treatment of the findings summarized in this section.

Counties Providing Less Than Four Years' Work

Of the remaining 1,128 counties, 528 provided less than four years of public secondary education for 274,000 Negroes of approximate high school age who resided therein in 1933.

This group included 25.6 per cent of all Negroes 15 to 19 years of age in the Southern states. Grouping these counties according to the most advanced public secondary work offered by the Negro schools within a given county, they may be divided as follows:

1. 190 counties entirely without public high school facilities.
2. 68 counties wherein public schools provide one year only, of secondary work.
3. 153 counties wherein public schools offer but two years of high school work.
3. 117 counties wherein public schools are located, providing not more than three years of work at the secondary level.

Arkansas (57.9 per cent), Mississippi (50.5 per cent), Georgia (45.0 per cent), South Carolina (24.9 per cent), Florida (24.4 per cent), Alabama (23.2 per cent) and Louisiana (20.9 per cent) were states having more than 20 per cent of their total Negro high school population living in counties wherein less than four-year public secondary facilities were provided.

North Carolina (2.7 per cent), Maryland (3.9 per cent), West Virginia (8.3 per cent), Tennessee (11.9 per cent) and Texas (11.9 per cent) were states in the lower range.

The data indicate that there are some states wherein a great deal still needs to be done in stimulating public school authorities to provide at least one four-year public secondary school capable of doing creditable work. In these states carefully planned developmental programs consistent with the many correlative factors peculiar to the various counties and their constituencies should be worked out by public authorities and officers of those philanthropic agencies working to improve Negro education.

Counties Providing Four-Year Public Secondary Education for Negroes

1. There were 600 counties wherein one or more public schools provided four-year secondary facilities in 1933. Residing within these counties

were 791,300 Negroes of approximate high school age and as a group they constituted 73.9 per cent of all such persons living in the South.

2. Of these counties, 255 possessed at least one fully accredited four-year public secondary school.

In general, the probabilities in favor of the Negro student having some access to a four-year secondary school located in the county wherein he resides decrease as the total Negro 15 to 19 years age group increases in a given state.

These findings are pregnant with suggestions for future activity in developing Negro secondary education. That 73.9 per cent of the Negro population (15 to 19 years of age) in the South resided in counties providing four-year public secondary facilities, and that only 15 per cent were enrolled in these schools, is a serious indictment. It has been shown that the secondary grades in Negro schools are not over-crowded in general, especially in rural schools. We have seen the demand for secondary education on the part of Negroes reflected in the many one- and two-year schools trying to meet this cry for more advanced educational facilities. The matter narrows to a problem of making accessible to greater numbers that which is already more or less available.

Several possible alternative corrective means can be mentioned. Boarding facilities could be provided but those concerned with County Training Schools have found that fewer and fewer pupils are utilizing the dormitory facilities provided in certain of these schools.

It is more than likely that in certain large counties, thickly populated with Negroes and wherein transportation seems impracticable, at least one four-year high school could provide living accommodations to take care of students coming from smaller secondary schools strategically placed with respect to centers of Negro concentration. This presupposes a carefully organized and well supervised county system of schools. The smaller schools could be organized on a 6-2 or 6-3 plan but the work would have to be of approved secondary merit and carefully articulated with that of the central school so as to facilitate easy transfer. South Carolina, Florida, and possibly one or two other states could utilize profitably such a scheme.

Many counties have Training Schools which could serve as larger central schools, but few, if any, have any organized system of "feeder" or smaller secondary schools.

On the other hand there could be established more small four-year secondary schools located close to the Negro population clusters within counties. Facts indicate that pupil-costs increase and the quality and scope of educational offering decrease in the smaller high schools. The difficulties, however, are not insurmountable and there is a determined group of educators attacking the problem of the enrichment of the small secondary curriculum without appreciably increasing costs.

Another alternative is to provide transportation to a far greater extent than is now practiced and perhaps contemplated. Here again are obstacles. Transportation is expensive, at least in the initial stages and often thereafter. It usually involves consolidation and this is often impracticable, due to topographical, socio-psychological, political, and other reasons. It has worked, however, with notable success, even in Negro education. Outstanding in this respect is the case of Warren County, North Carolina. With 15,000 Negroes constituting two-thirds of the total population, fifteen buses were secured by the Negroes with the aid of the Rosenwald Fund. The county and state educational authorities provide for maintenance. With the exception of a small portion of the county having only paths for roads, every section can offer its Negro youth public secondary facilities.

There is still another important consideration concerned with these four-year secondary schools; that of better articulation with the Negro higher institutions. There is a growing demand for improving the quality of the educational product of Negro secondary schools. Consequently there is need for careful and sensible accrediting of these secondary schools. Frequently the resources of a community are barely equal to the task of maintaining the four-year secondary school they possess. Often a small amount of aid carries such schools a long way toward the goal of accredited status.

Obviously, here are several opportunities for agencies interested in improving Negro secondary education. The example set by Warren County is sufficiently suggestive in itself.

Summary and Interpretation

Some one ought to sponsor an attempt to determine just what can be done with a group of small secondary schools so organized and administered as to try out methods and techniques adapted, not to large urban schools, but to small rural high schools.

THE PLACE OF COUNTY TRAINING SCHOOLS IN THE PUBLIC NEGRO SECONDARY FIELD[4]

This movement is considered by some authorities as one of the most important developments in Negro education in recent times. The results presented here should indicate, with a considerable degree of accuracy, the extent to which these schools may be considered factors in the scheme of public secondary education for Negroes. The more important findings and conclusions, together with interpretations and a few of the supporting data follow:

The County Training Schools Aided During 1932-33

The data indicate that the County Training School movement is of wide geographical spread and educational range and consequently is of more than ordinary importance.

1. During 1932-33, 356 schools in 352 counties in 14 Southern states were aided by the Slater Fund. Over 170,000 pupils were enrolled in these schools, 16,389 of whom were in the secondary grades. The teaching force aggregated 2,601 persons, 936 of whom devoted their full time to the high school subjects.

Thus it can be stated that 11 per cent of all Negro high school pupils and 17.7 per cent of all full-time teachers in public secondary schools for Negroes in the South were in County Training Schools being cooperatively sponsored by public school authorities and the John F. Slater Fund, in 1932-33.

The percentage of each state's total secondary enrollment found in County Training Schools varied greatly. Louisiana (26.8 per cent) and Mississippi (23.7 per cent) represented one extreme and Missouri (1.7 per cent) and Oklahoma (2.7 per cent) were indicative of the other.

2. In 205 counties the County Training School being aided was the only public secondary school to which the Negro constituency could send their children for this level of education.

[4]See Chapter IV for detailed treatment of the findings summarized in this section.

This is perhaps the strongest single piece of evidence indicative of the importance of the movement. No device for measurement can describe in objective terms the significance of County Training Schools to Negroes who actually live in counties where the line between *have* and *have not* in secondary education is so thinly drawn.

County Training Schools: Past and Present

The cumulative extent of the movement and the actual place these schools occupy in the public Negro secondary field were ascertained by a careful study of all County Training Schools aided by the Fund from 1911 through 1933. The results obtained follow:

1. Distribution of County Training Schools.
   a. County Training Schools are most numerous in the states having the larger Negro populations and are located so as to be of potential service to the majority of this group.

The evidence shows that of the 612 schools identified with the County Training School movement during the years 1911 to 1933, 75 per cent are located in the eight states having the largest Negro populations of approximate high school age. These states (Alabama, Georgia, Louisiana, Mississippi, North Carolina, South Carolina, Texas and Virginia) possess 77 per cent of the total Negro population of the South. Of the 459 schools located in these states, 73 per cent are found in the open country or in small rural villages and towns.

   b. The majority of County Training Schools have developed into schools offering four years of secondary work, and these are found mostly in rural localities.

Out of 612 schools, 399 provided four-year courses of study in 1933. Two hundred thirty of these four-year schools are located in rural communities.

Arkansas, Mississippi and South Carolina are the only states wherein less than 50 per cent of their Training Schools have developed into four-year schools.

Florida, Kentucky and Tennessee deviate from the general tendency since the majority of the County Training Schools indicate an urban location. This may be due to the evolution of small towns into urban communities. It is not strictly true of Florida since most of the schools are located in large cities.

Summary and Interpretation

c. County Training Schools carry a large share of the responsibility for providing public secondary school facilities for Negroes in the South.

The data show that 30.5 per cent of all public secondary schools included in this study have at one time been identified with the County Training School movement. At the same time these Training Schools include only 7.7 per cent of the 1-year schools, 20 per cent of the 2-year schools, and 26 per cent of the 3-year schools. This signifies that few of the less desirable small schools attempting to stretch their limited educational resources into the high school grades are included in the Training School group. The distribution of 4-year schools shows that 59.3 per cent of all such schools in rural areas and 40.3 per cent of the 4-year urban schools are County Training Schools.

2. The Accredited Training Schools.
    a. Of the 399 four-year County Training Schools 181 were fully accredited and they enrolled 20,085 pupils in the secondary grades in 1933. These figures do not include 31 Parish Training Schools in Louisiana, which have been State approved on a basis slightly lower than the accredited standards.
    b. Accredited Training Schools are smaller than non-Slater-aided accredited schools.

While 49.4 per cent of all accredited Negro schools have been at some time identified with the Training School movement they enroll but 25 per cent of the high school students found in the 367 accredited schools included in this investigation. The average accredited County Training School enrolls 116 pupils. It is an interesting fact that 80 per cent of the accredited Training Schools are located in rural communities. There is a suggestion of utmost significance to educators implied in this evidence. In so far as accrediting stands for desirable qualitative standards, it has been demonstrated that small rural high schools *can* offer excellent secondary work.

The Slater Fund does not assist schools after they have attained four-year state accredited status.

3. The Enrollment and Size of Training Schools.
    a. The students enrolled in the secondary grades of County Training Schools constituted 31.2 per cent of all Negroes who enrolled in public schools offering secondary work in the South.

    b. In so far as the size of a school is determined by enrollment, Training Schools are generally larger than the non-Slater-aided public secondary schools.

The average enrollment per school in County Training Schools was higher in all rural one-year, two-year, three-year and four-year schools than in the non-Slater-aided rural schools. In only the three-year and four-year urban schools were the non-Slater-aided schools larger in size. Nevertheless, Negro secondary schools are small and if it is true that the problems of secondary schools become more acute as their enrollments decrease then administrators of Negro schools need to approach the problems of secondary schools armed with a full knowledge of their smallness.

4. The Secondary Teachers in County Training Schools.
    a. Thirty-three per cent of all public Negro secondary school teachers were found in County Training Schools.
    b. The Slater-aided one-year, two-year and three-year schools have larger secondary teaching forces than the non-Slater-aided public schools. The pupil-teacher ratio also is higher in the County Training Schools. The difference is not great except in the one-year schools where the non-Slater-aided schools have but one-half as large a pupil-teacher ratio.
    c. The average non-Slater-aided four-year school has more teachers than the average County Training School in that class. This might be taken to indicate that the problem of providing an adequate secondary program is more serious, in these four-year County Training Schools since fewer teachers means employing the services of each teacher in a greater number of subject fields.
    d. Of the County Training Schools, only in the 190 *urban* schools providing three or four years of secondary work does the average number of pupils-per-teacher approach the 25 to 1 ratio considered by most authorities to be economically expedient.

In the non-Training-School group the one- and two-year schools are farther below the desirable pupil-teacher ratio than the County Training Schools in the same classification. On the other hand the average number of pupils per teacher in the three- and four-year urban non-Slater-aided schools tends to exceed the economically desirable ratio.

This broadly signifies that if there is over-crowding in public secondary schools for Negroes, in so far as pupil-teacher ratios are concerned, the cases will most frequently occur in the 290 non-Slater-aided urban three and four-year schools. The most important implication, however, is that public Negro secondary schools are generally not over-crowded; in fact, their pupil-teacher ratios are generally not economically sound.

COUNTY TRAINING SCHOOLS AND PUBLIC SECONDARY EDUCATIONAL PROVISION FOR NEGROES[5]

Schools identified at some time with the County Training School movement are located in 517 counties in 15 southern states. The movement, consequently, embraces 56.7 per cent of all counties in the South which provided some public high school education for Negroes in 1933. Most of these County Training Schools represent an original cooperative effort, in a given county, to develop at least one school into secondary status or perhaps to encourage a particular school to offer more advanced high school work. An inquiry into the extent to which these schools are still providing the only, or most advanced, public secondary work should yield two results. It should indicate the place these schools have in the public Negro secondary field and it should disclose to some extent the progress certain states have made in providing for their Negro secondary educables. The following are the more significant findings and interpretations consequent to this phase of the investigation:

1. When 44.2 per cent of all Negroes 15 to 19 years of age residing in counties in the South wherein some public high school work is offered, live in counties where the only, or most advanced, public secondary facilities available are those provided by County Training Schools there can be no doubt as to their significance. The evidence indicates that for the ambitious Negro secondary student the Training Schools constitute an inestimable educational asset. A very real problem, nevertheless, exists in making them more accessible to greater numbers.

The supporting data are of more than corroborative value since they add reality to the connotations of the previous statement. They follow:

a. In 293 counties in 15 states the only schools providing any public secondary facilities for Negroes were County Training Schools. The Negro population 15 to 19 years of age in these counties aggregated 281,245 persons. Of this number 7.8 per cent were enrolled in the secondary grades. In 198 counties

[5]See Chapter IV for detailed treatment of the findings summarized in this section.

the Training School provided four years of secondary work.
   b. There were, in addition to these counties, 104 others wherein the most advanced secondary work available to 155,500 Negroes of approximate high school age was provided by County Training Schools. There were enrolled in these schools 10,382 pupils. In 89 cases the schools offered four years of high school work.
2. While great variability characterizes the percentages indicative of the extent to which Negroes in the several states need to seek their only, or most advanced, public secondary education in County Training Schools, the states having the greater Negro populations tend to depend most upon these schools in the sense indicated above.

Since the Training School movement has been largely centered in the more densely Negro populated states these findings are not surprising. When, however, unmistakable exceptions to the general tendency appear it nominates them for particular consideration. In this respect,—

   a. Arkansas (71.7 per cent), Florida (48.4 per cent) and Kentucky (41.2 per cent) with high percentages of dependency on schools included in the County Training School category and with relatively small Negro populations, stand out.
   b. On the other hand Texas (23.3 per cent) and North Carolina (30.5 per cent) with relatively low percentages of dependency upon County Training Schools and with decidedly large Negro populations are also conspicuous.

A previous conclusion pointed out that states possessing the larger Negro constituencies tended to enroll the lower percentages of their respective Negro high school population. Here again Arkansas (6.9 per cent) and Florida (12 per cent) were the less desirable exceptions, while Texas (24.4 per cent) and North Carolina (20.0 per cent) represented the opposite deviations. Kentucky (24.6 per cent) was exceeded only by Oklahoma (31.3 per cent) and Missouri (27.7 per cent) in the percentage of their respective Negro high school populations enrolled in public secondary schools.

The evidence points very strongly to the conclusion that Arkansas and Florida, in view of the size of their Negro constituencies, do not compare favorably with other Southern states with respect to the provisions made for public secondary education of Negroes. Undoubtedly, many unpredictable factors not specifically included in this investigation, are responsible.

Summary and Interpretation 113

3. Despite the fact that many Negroes of approximate high school age in Arkansas (71.7 per cent) and Florida (48.4 per cent) live in counties wherein they must depend largely on County Training Schools for secondary educational opportunities, these schools indicate an evolution inconsistent with comparative developmental tendencies evidenced in other states. This is tantamount to saying that the development has been inconsistent with the general aims and policies of those who sponsored them.

The data indicate that in Florida seventeen out of twenty-three schools aided at some time by the Slater Fund as County Training Schools are located in large towns or cities. All of the four year schools are so located. While not entirely conclusive, the data which are available indicate that the amount of transportation provided at public expense, does not make these urban schools available to any considerable proportion of the rural secondary population in the counties wherein these schools are located. Few of the County Training Schools in Arkansas have developed into four-year secondary schools and most of those that have attained this status are located in urban places.

4. The evidence reveals that no other states in the South, which possessed Negro secondary populations of more than 40,000 persons, enrolled more of their Negro educables in public secondary schools than North Carolina and Texas in 1933.

In both states the County Training School movement has been very active.

5. Tennessee, Virginia, Louisiana, South Carolina, Alabama, Mississippi and Georgia tend to rely greatly on the County Training Schools to provide public secondary facilities for Negro students. With the exception of Tennessee and Virginia, these states possess many counties with considerable Negro populations, providing little or no high school facilities for their inhabitants.

State Recognition of County Training Schools[6]

1. With the exception of North Carolina, no state has passed any legislation specifically providing for County Training School establishment. Evidently laws and statutes operative in the establishment of elementary and high schools served as adequate legal bases for County Training Schools.
2. From time to time state educational authorities have endorsed the County Training School movement and official recognition of it has been included in the authoritative publications of the Southern states.

[6] See Chapter IV for detailed treatment of the findings summarized in this section.

RECOMMENDATIONS

1. This investigation revealed that there were at least 190 counties in the South entirely without public secondary educational facilities for Negroes in 1933.[7] It is recommended that local, county, state, and philanthropic agencies cooperate in a determined effort to reduce the number of such counties. The complete elimination of counties in this category should be the ultimate objective.

2. It is recommended that local, county, state, and philanthropic agencies cooperate in an attempt to eliminate, as rapidly as possible, the secondary work being offered in the many small elementary schools which do not possess adequate facilities for providing acceptable secondary work.

3. One finding growing out of this study revealed that the majority of public high schools for Negroes are not overcrowded in the secondary grades. On the contrary it was indicated that many schools could accommodate more high school pupils without exceeding the economically desirable pupil-teacher ratio. At the same time it was shown that a relatively small per cent of the Negroes of high school age were enrolled in these secondary grades.

It is recommended, therefore, that local, county, state, and philanthropic agencies cooperate in making available to greater numbers of Negro students the educational opportunities offered in schools already established and functioning as desirable public secondary schools.

4. In view of the findings concerning the many counties[8] possessing one or more public schools offering less than four years of secondary work for Negroes, it is recommended that local, county, state, and philanthropic agencies cooperate in developing at least one four-year school per county capable of providing acceptable or accredited secondary work; and that this school should be open to children from all parts of the county.

Based solely upon personal impressions gained from field trips and discussions with officials engaged in administering Negro education it is suggested that a reasonable sum of money

---

[7]The identities of such counties and their Negro populations of high school age are included in Appendix C.

[8]See Appendix C for specific information concerning these counties.

be placed at the disposal of State Agents for Negro Education to be used in stimulating the development of promising and deserving schools toward attaining the desirable four-year status.

5. It was found that certain of the County Training Schools have not developed in a manner consistent with the aims and policies of those who sponsored them. It is therefore suggested that an investigation be undertaken by the agencies interested in these schools to ascertain the developmental possibilities of the schools that are now being sponsored.

In light of the great need for stimulating the development of public secondary facilities for Negroes it would seem advisable to discontinue aid to schools which are unlikely to develop into acceptable four-year status and to apply the stimulative effort and assistance elsewhere.

It would probably make for more definite development if local, county, state, and philanthropic agencies cooperated in a careful study of factors that affect: future availability or accessibility, intra- and inter-county cooperation, population dispersion, and such sociological considerations as seem important, before encouraging secondary development in any locality.

6. It is recommended that local, county, state and philanthropic agencies recognize the fact that public secondary schools for Negroes, with few exceptions, are small.

Such recognition should be expressed in practical administration as follows:

a. By encouraging an investigation of certain small rural and urban accredited secondary schools to discover what characteristics, factors, methods and techniques may be of suggestive and practical value for other secondary schools in the process of development.

b. By suggesting that local, county, state, and philanthropic agencies establish and maintain at least one experimental small high school for Negroes in each of the Southern states as a means of discovering desirable information for use in further secondary development.

c. By encouraging some central agency, so situated as to have direct relations with responsible authorities in Negro education, to bring to the attention of these officials such pertinent information as would enable them more effectively to stimulate desirable development in secondary Negro education.

The United States Office of Education functioning through the office of the Senior Specialist in Education for Negroes should be enabled to expand the worthy beginnings already made in this direction and adequate means for performing this service should be provided. If this proves impossible it may then become necessary to set up a new agency to serve as a clearing house and vigorous disseminator of information about Negro education.

Bibliography

I. OFFICIAL PROCEEDINGS AND REPORTS

DILLARD, JAMES HARDY. "County Training Schools," *Report to the Trustees of the John F. Slater Fund,* 1920. On file in the office of the Slater Fund, 726 Jackson Place, N. W., Washington, D. C.

THE GENERAL EDUCATION BOARD. *Annual Reports of the General Education Board,* 1902-1914; 1921-22; 1922-23; 1924-25. General Education Board, 61 Broadway, New York City.

JOHN F. SLATER FUND. *Proceedings and Reports.* For years ending, September 30, 1910 through 1929. For years ending June 30, 1930 through 1934.

These are the official reports of the President of the Slater Fund and contain much information concerning the relation of the Fund to the development of County Training Schools for Negroes. Available in printed form. Inquire, John F. Slater Fund, 726 Jackson Place, N. W., Washington, D. C.

THE PHELPS-STOKES FUND. *Educational Adaptations.* Report of the Phelps-Stokes Fund 1910-1920. The Phelps-Stokes Fund, 1920, Office: 101 Park Avenue, New York City.

THE PHELPS-STOKES FUND. *Twenty Year Report of the Phelps-Stokes Fund,* 1911-1931. The Phelps-Stokes Fund, 1932, Office: 101 Park Avenue, New York City.

A discussion of general conditions in Negro education with a valuable delineation of trends. Sections contributed by Dr. Thomas Jesse Jones, Dr. James Hardy Dillard, Dr. C. T. Loram and others.

II. AUDIT SHEETS

STATISTICAL REPORTS OF THE JOHN F. SLATER FUND, 1919 to 1932. On file in the office of the Fund, 726 Jackson Place, N. W., Washington, D. C.

III. PAPERS AND PAMPHLETS

TRUSTEES OF THE JOHN F. SLATER FUND. *Documents Relating to the Origin and Work of the Slater Trustees.* Occasional Papers, No. 1, 1894, The Slater Fund, Washington, D. C.

TRUSTEES OF THE JOHN F. SLATER FUND. *A Brief Memoir of the Life of John F. Slater.* Occasional Papers, No. 2, The Slater Fund, Washington, D. C., 1894.

TRUSTEES OF THE JOHN F. SLATER FUND. *County Training Schools for Negroes.* Occasional Papers, No. 14, The Slater Fund, Washington, D. C., 1913.

A short pamphlet sent to State and County Superintendents in the South, to obtain opinions concerning the development of central training schools for Negroes.

TRUSTEES OF THE JOHN F. SLATER FUND. *Suggested Course of Study for County Training Schools.* Occasional Papers, No. 18, The Slater Fund, Washington, D. C., 1917.

TRUSTEES OF THE JOHN F. SLATER FUND. *County Training Schools for Negroes.* Occasional Papers, No. 23, The Slater Fund, Washington, D. C., 1923.

Leo M. Favrot studied the County Training Schools in 1921. It is the only specific study made of these schools to date. The study considered status, curriculum, achievement and retardation of pupils and opinions of educators concerning these schools.

TRUSTEES OF THE JOHN F. SLATER FUND. *Public Secondary Schools for Negroes in the Southern States of the United States.* Occasional Papers, No. 29, The John F. Slater Fund, Washington, D. C., 1935.

McCUISTION, FRED. *Financing Schools in the South.* State Directors of Education Research, 502 Cotton States Building, Nashville, Tennessee, 1930.

One of the first studies of financing of public education in the South pointing attention to two important facts: the Southern states are poor (financially) and their efforts to educate the Negro are not commensurate with their ability to educate.

IV. GOVERNMENT PUBLICATIONS

CALIVER, AMBROSE. *A Background Study of Negro College Students.* United States Bureau of Education Bulletin No. 8, 1933. Government Printing Office, Washington, D. C.

CALIVER, AMBROSE. *Secondary Education for Negroes.* United States Bureau of Education Bulletin, No. 17, Government Printing Office, Washington, D. C., 1932.

This is the section of the National Survey of Secondary Education devoted to Negro secondary education. It is the most comprehensive study of this field of education in the Southern states since Dr. Thomas Jesse Jones' study of 1915. The portion of the study presenting the "Status" of secondary education for Negroes would be better if more nearly complete data had been available.

CALIVER, AMBROSE. *Rural Elementary Education Among Negroes Under Jeanes Supervising Teachers.* United States Office of Education Bulletin, 1933, No. 5, Government Printing Office, Washington, D. C.

COOK, KATHERINE M. *Biennial Survey of Education in the United States, 1929-30.* United States Bureau of Education Bulletin No. 20, Government Printing Office, Washington, D. C., 1931.

A valuable bulletin presenting statistical facts and recommendations concerning the education of certain racial groups in the

Bibliography 119

United States and its territories. Messrs. John H. McBride, Jr., W. Carson Ryan, Jr., William Hamilton and Ambrose Caliver collaborated in the preparation of this document.

FERRISS, EMERY N., GAUMNITZ, W. H., and BRAMMELL, ROY P. *The Smaller Secondary Schools*. United States Bureau of Education Bulletin, 1932, No. 17, Monograph No. 6, Government Printing Office, Washington, D. C.

GAUMNITZ, WALTER H. *The Smallness of America's Rural High Schools*. United States Bureau of Education Bulletin, 1930, No. 13, Government Printing Office, Washington, D. C.

JONES, THOMAS JESSE. *Negro Education: A Study of Private and Higher Schools for Colored People in the United States*. United States Bureau of Education Bulletins, Nos. 38 and 39, Government Printing Office, Washington, D. C., 1916.

A most comprehensive study of Negro Education, undertaken at a time when little or nothing definite was available with reference to the South as a section. It is a milestone from which recent progress in secondary and higher Negro education is measured.

JONES, THOMAS JESSE. *Recent Progress in Negro Education*. United States Bureau of Education Bulletin, No. 27, Government Printing Office, Washington, D. C., 1919.

SPAULDING, FRANCIS T., FREDERICK, O. I., and KOOS, LEONARD. *The Reorganization of Secondary Education*. United States Bureau of Education Bulletin, 1932, No. 17, Monograph No. 5, Government Printing Office, Washington, D. C.

V. PUBLICATIONS OF STATE DEPARTMENTS OF EDUCATION

ALLEN, A. T. *Biennial Report of the Superintendent of Public Instruction of North Carolina*. For the scholastic years 1928, 1929, Raleigh, North Carolina.

BOND, W. F. *Biennial Reports of the State Superintendent of Public Education of Mississippi*. For the scholastic years, 1921-1923 and 1923-1925, Jackson, Mississippi.

BRITTAIN, M. L. *Forty-fourth Annual Report of the Department of Education of the State of Georgia*. For the Biennium ending June 30, 1932, Atlanta, Georgia.

BROOKS, E. C. *The Public School Law of North Carolina*. Codification of 1923. State Department of Education, Raleigh, North Carolina.

BROWN, J. B. *Annual Report of the State Superintendent of Public Instruction of Tennessee*. For the scholastic year ending June 30, 1922, Nashville, Tennessee.

CAWTHON, W. S. *Biennial Report of the Superintendent of Public Instruction of the State of Florida*. For the year ending June 30, 1932, Tallahassee, Florida.

COLVIN, G. *Report of the Superintendent of Public Instruction of Kentucky.* For two years ending June 30, 1921.

DUGGAN, MELL L. *Sixty-first Report of the Department of Education of Georgia.* For the Biennium ending June 30, 1932, Atlanta, Georgia.

FEAGIN, W. F. *Annual Report of the State Department of Education of Alabama.* Montgomery, Alabama, for the scholastic year ending September 30, 1916.

HALL, SIDNEY B. *Annual Report of the Superintendent of Public Instruction of Virginia.* Richmond, Virginia. School year, 1931-1932.

HARMAN, A. F. *Annual Report of the State Department of Education of Alabama.* Montgomery, Alabama, for the year ending June, 1931.

HARRIS, T. H. *Annual Report of the State Superintendent of Public Education of Louisiana.* Baton Rouge, Louisiana, for the session 1925-1926.

HARRIS, T. H. *Eightieth Annual Report of the State Superintendent of Public Education of Louisiana.* Baton Rouge, Louisiana, for the session 1928-1929.

HART, HARRIS. *Annual Report of the Superintendent of Public Instruction of Virginia.* Richmond, Virginia, school year 1923-1924.

HIRST, C. M. *Biennial Report of the State Commissioner of Education of Arkansas.* Little Rock, Arkansas, 1930-1932.

HOPE, JAMES H. *Sixty-Fifth Annual Report of the State Superintendent of Education of the State of South Carolina.* Columbia, South Carolina, for the school session, 1932-33.

MARRS, S. M. N. *The Twenty-fourth Biennial Report of the State Department of Education of Texas.* Austin, Texas, 1924-26.

MARRS, S. M. N.; BLUDWORTH, G. T., and TAYLOR, D. B. *Negro Education in Texas.* Bulletin, No. 294, State Department of Education, Austin Texas, 1931.

SHERRILL, S. W. *Biennial Report of the State Superintendent of Public Instruction of Tennessee.* Nashville, Tennessee, for the scholastic year ending 1917-1918.

STEARNS, R. C. *Annual Report of the Superintendent of Public Instruction of Virginia.* Richmond, Virginia, School year 1917-1918,

Valuable information relative to the work of the Slater Fund in specific states is incorporated in these official statements of state authorities.

VI. ARTICLES ON NEGRO EDUCATION

CALDWELL, B. C. "The Work of the Jeanes and Slater Funds," *The Annals of the American Academy of Political and Social Science,* Vol. No. 36, pp. 172-177.

This article briefly sketches certain phases of the beginnings of the County Training School project. B. C. Caldwell was the Field Agent of the Slater Fund in 1913.

DILLARD, JAMES HARDY. "School Helps in the Open Country," *Opportunity*, Vol. 1, No. 3, pp. 10-12, 1923.

DILLARD, JAMES HARDY. "A Happy Development," *Opportunity*, Vol. 8, January, 1930, pp. 14-16.

DUBOIS, W. E. B. "Education and Work," *The Journal of Negro Education*, Vol. 1, April, 1932, pp. 60-74.

FAVROT, LEO M. "Negro Education in the South, an Abstract," *Addresses and Proceedings of the National Education Association*, 58: 1920, pp. 291-296.

FAVROT, LEO M. "Some Facts About Negro High Schools and Their Distribution and Development in the Southern States," *High School Quarterly*, Vol. XVII, 1929, pp. 139-155.

JONES, THOMAS JESSE. "Frissell of Hampton," *Southern Workman*, Vol. 60, January, 1931, pp. 65-69.

Frissell was principal of Hampton Institute from 1893-1918 and his ideas are reflected in many ways in the education of Negroes in the South. This article is a good presentation of the man and his educational credo.

MOTON, ROBERT R. "Progress of Negro Education in the South," *Addresses and Proceedings of the National Education Association*, 1929, pp. 107-11.

Dr. Moton succeeded Booker T. Washington as Principal of Tuskegee Institute. The article is well worth reading since it reflects the experience of a Negro who has "lived close" to the educational progress of the race since 1880.

NEWBOLD, N. C. "Common Schools for Negroes in the South," *The Annals of the American Academy of Political and Social Science*, Vol. CXXXX, Philadelphia, 1928.

ROBINSON, W. A. "Four-Year State Accredited High Schools for Negroes in Seventeen Southern States," *Bulletin of the National Association of Teachers in Colored Schools*, Vol. VII, 1927, pp. 6-10.

ROBINSON, W. A. "Four-Year Accredited High School for Negroes in the South," *Bulletin of the National Association of Teachers in Colored Schools*, Vol. VIII, 1928, pp. 6-15.

SMITH, S. L. "Negro Public Schools in the South," *Southern Workman*, November, 1928.

TRIGG, H. L. "Sources and Comparative Data Relative to the Teaching Staff of North Carolina Accredited Negro High Schools for 1929-1930," *North Carolina Teachers Record*, Vol. 1, 1930, pp. 6-8.

TAYLOR, D. B. "Henderson County Training School, Malokoff, Texas," *Southern Workman*, Vol. 57, 1928, pp. 232-33.

WASHINGTON, BOOKER T. "Industrial Education, Public Schools and the Negroes," *Annals of the American Academy of Political and Social Science*, Vol. 49, September, 1913, pp. 219-32.

Booker T. Washington was one of the original corporation trustees of the Anna T. Jeanes Foundation and served as Chairman of its Executive Committee until his death. Dr. Dillard of the Slater Fund was also president of the Jeanes Foundation during this time. After reading this article one sees a possible genesis of Dr. Dillard's ideas pertaining to County Training Schools for Negroes.

WORK, MONROE N. "Tuskegee Institute More Than An Educational Institution," *The Journal of Education Sociology*, Vol. VII, No. 3, November, 1933, p. 197.

The entire contents of this issue of the *Journal* are devoted to Negro education. Articles were submitted by Robert R. Moton, Alphonse Heningburg, William A. Clark, W. T. B. Williams, Russell C. Atkins, Monroe N. Work and others.

VII. GENERAL WORKS

BRAWLEY, BENJAMIN. *Doctor Dillard of the Jeanes Fund.* Fleming H. Revell, Company, New York City, 1930.

CYR, FRANK W. (Editor) *Economical Enrichment of the Small Secondary School Curriculum.* The Department of Rural Education, National Education Association, Washington, D. C., 1934.

DAVIS, W. R. *The Development and Present Status of Negro Education in East Texas.* Bureau of Publications, Teachers College, Columbia University, New York, N. Y., 1934.

A short section of this study is devoted to the County Training School movement in Texas.

HOLMES, D. O. W. *Evolution of the Negro College.* Bureau of Publications, Teachers College, Columbia University, New York City, 1934.

JOHNSON, CHARLES S. *The Negro in American Civilization.* Henry Holt, New York, 1932.

This sociologist from Fiske University has gathered what is said to be the finest collection of sociological data on the Negro in the United States, if not the world. A compilation and synthesis of many studies dealing with various aspects of Negro life, growing out of the work of the National Inter-racial Conference.

JONES, LANCE G. E. *Negro Schools in the Southern States.* The Clarendon Press, Oxford, England, 1928.

An English educator, after an extended tour of the Southern states, writes a general account of education for Negroes as he found it. Dr. Jones' comments are stimulating and his criticism on the whole, seems justified. A good book for anyone interested in Negro education.

LEAVELL, ULLIN W. *Philanthropy in Negro Education.* Contribution to Education No. 100, George Peabody College for Teachers, Cullom and Ghertner Company, Nashville, Tennessee, 1930.

Bibliography

LONG, H. M. *Public Secondary Education for Negroes in North Carolina.* Bureau of Publications, Teachers College, Columbia University, New York, 1932.

MCCUISTION, FRED. *The South's Negro Teaching Force.* The Julius Rosenwald Fund, Nashville, Tennessee, 1931.

MOTON, ROBERT R. *What the Negro Thinks.* Doubleday, Doran and Company, Inc., Garden City, New York, 1929.

Why the Negro smiles when the white person says "I know the Negro." The writer shows you that there are vast reaches of Negro life and thought of which white people know very little.

NOBLE, STUART G. *Forty Years of the Public Schools in Mississippi.* Bureau of Publications, Teachers College, Columbia University, New York, N. Y., 1918.

ODELL, W. R. *Gifts to the Public Schools.* W. R. Odell, Publisher, 525 West 120th Street, New York City, 1932.

WORK, MONROE N. *Negro Year Book.* Negro Year Book Publishing Company, Tuskegee Institute, Alabama, 1931-1932.

This handbook provides elaborate and exact material concerning the Negro and is an indispensable source for any student of race problems.

WOODSON, CARTER G. *The Education of the Negro Prior to 1861.* G. P. Putnam's Sons, New York, 1915.

A history of the education of Negroes in the United States from the early beginnings of Slavery to the Civil War.

WOODSON, CARTER G. *The Negro in Our History.* Associated Publishers, Washington, D. C., 1928.

WOODSON, CARTER G. *The Mis-Education of the Negro.* Associated Publishers, Washington, D. C., 1933.

A pointed and fearless criticism of the education of Negroes in the United States in which both white and Negro leaders and administrators are considered.

WOOFTER, T. J. JR. *Races and Ethnic Groups in American Life.* McGraw-Hill Book Company, 1933.

A compilation of monographs published under the direction of the President's Research Committee on Social Trends and limited to the consideration of needs rather than an exposition of the present situation. The title of the series, "Recent Social Trends Monographs" indicates the nature of the work.

WRIGHT, ARTHUR D. *The Negro Rural School Fund, Inc. (Anna T. Jeanes Foundation),* 1907-1933. Published by the Negro Rural School Fund, Inc., Washington, D. C.

WRIGHTSTONE, J. C. *Stimulation of Educational Undertakings—A Study of School Support in New York City* and *Villages Under Earmarked* and *Non-Earmarked State Subsidy Plans.* Bureau of Publications, Teachers College, Columbia University, New York City, 1933.

YOUNG, DONALD. *American Minority Peoples.* Harper Brothers, New York, 1932.

An impartial analysis and interpretation of facts and principles of researches in race relations carried on since 1914. It is an objective and scientifically written document and is a valuable source for the serious student seeking an adequate knowledge of the problems of race conflict and misunderstanding.

APPENDIXES

APPENDIX A
THE QUESTIONNAIRE

Obverse Side:
    Reply Card.
    This side is for address.

    The John F. Slater Fund,
    726 Jackson Place, N. W.,
    Washington, D. C.

September 15, 1933.

For more than 20 years the John F. Slater Fund has been making an effort to assist in the development of a system of public secondary schools for Negroes in the Southern States. We now feel that it would be advantageous to have complete data in regard to such schools and to that end we ask you to fill out and mail the attached stamped card at your earliest convenience. Will you please give the requested data as of the school year, 1932-1933? If no high school work for Negroes is offered in your county or city, will you please sign and return the card indicating that fact?

Thanking you in advance for your cooperation, I am,

Sincerely yours,

ARTHUR D. WRIGHT,
President, John F. Slater Fund.

THE QUESTIONNAIRE

Reverse Side:
County.......................... State..........................
(Please list all schools under your jurisdiction offering any High School work for Negroes).

Name of School	P. O. Address	Principal
1.		
2.		
3.		
4.		

No. Years H. S. Work Offered	No. Full Time H. S. Teachers	No. Part Time H. S. Teachers	Total Enrollment of Entire School	Enrollment in Specific Grades:					
				7	8	9	10	11	12
1.									
2.									
3.									
4.									

(Signed)..........................Superintendent.

APPENDIX B‡

TABLE 1

ENROLLMENT AND NUMBER OF TEACHERS IN PUBLIC SCHOOLS OFFERING 1 YEAR OF SECONDARY WORK FOR NEGROES IN 17 SOUTHERN STATES AND THE DISTRICT OF COLUMBIA, 1932-33.

State	Number of Schools			Enrollment			Number of Teachers		
	Rural	Urban	Total	Rural	Urban	Total	Full Time	Part Time	Total
Alabama	47	11	58	280	354	634	17	57	74
Arkansas	20	8†	28	217	62	279	11	27	38
Delaware	2		2	24		24	2		2
Florida	9	4	13	86	20	106	5	11	16
Georgia	46	5	51	259	374	633	16	45	61
Kentucky	1	3	4	8	535*	543	22*	1	23
Louisiana	4	2	6	45	21	66	3	4	7
Maryland		3	3		731*	731	24*		24
Mississippi	30	3	33	263	74	337	12	21	33
Missouri	1		1	10		10	1		1
North Carolina	13	2	15	135	25	160	5	12	17
Oklahoma	1		1	12		12	0	1	1
South Carolina	81	1	82	686	24	710	11	75	86
Tennessee	1		1	21		21	1	1	2
Texas	74	12	86	433	354	787	21	83	104
Virginia	5		5	121		121	3	2	5
West Virginia	5	3	8	184	227	411	8	19	27
District of Columbia		5	5		1,114*	1,114	36*		36
Total	340	62	402	2,784	3,915	6,699	198	359	557

* These figures are for the last year of junior high schools in city systems.

† Data incomplete for 3 schools in Arkansas but included in this table.

‡All data presented in this appendix were collected and compiled by the author.

TABLE 2
ENROLLMENT AND NUMBER OF TEACHERS IN PUBLIC SCHOOLS OFFERING 2 YEARS OF SECONDARY WORK FOR NEGROES IN 17 SOUTHERN STATES AND THE DISTRICT OF COLUMBIA, 1932-33

State	Number of Schools			Enrollment			Number of Teachers		
	Rural	Urban	Total	Rural	Urban	Total	Full Time	Part Time	Total
Alabama	5	13	18	143	281	424	12	22	34
Arkansas	12	8	20	189	209	398	17	17	34
Delaware									
Florida	3	10	13	60	213	273	14	23	37
Georgia	62	9	71	1060	370	1430	46	54	100
Kentucky	12	2	14	175	43	220	12	7	19
Louisiana	7	2	9	104	39	143	9	6	15
Maryland	2	1	3	73	33	106	3	1	4
Mississippi	43	4	47	1,044	116	1,160	49	39	88
Missouri	2	8	10	28	92	120	8	5	13
North Carolina	31	1	32	644	164	808	32	6	38
Oklahoma	6	1	7	94	12	106	10	3	13
South Carolina	51	5	56	810	186	996	27	49	76
Tennessee	16	10	26	439	540	979	29	24	53
Texas	106	11	117	1,125	197	1,322	36	91	127
Virginia	11	4	15	301	170	471	19	5	24
West Virginia	4		4	55		55	4	2	6
District of Columbia									
Total	373	89	462	6,344	2,667	9,011	327	354	681

TABLE 3
ENROLLMENT AND NUMBER OF TEACHERS IN PUBLIC SCHOOLS OFFERING 3 YEARS OF SECONDARY WORK FOR NEGROES IN 17 SOUTHERN STATES AND THE DISTRICT OF COLUMBIA, 1932-33

State	Number of Schools			Enrollment			Number of Teachers		
	Rural	Urban	Total	Rural	Urban	Total	Full Time	Part Time	Total
Alabama	6*	2	8	236	113	349	12	9	21
Arkansas	7	3	10	257	141	398	14	12	26
Delaware	2		2	70		70	2		2
Florida		1	1		40	40	2	1	3
Georgia	27	3	30	540	165	705	31	17	48
Kentucky	8	3	11	188	60	248	11	9	20
Louisiana	6	5	11	132	1,998	2,131	57	10	67
Maryland									
Mississippi	11	7	18	415	410	825	31	14	45
Missouri	2	1	3	80	16	96	5		5
North Carolina	26	2	28	1,084	235	1,319	43	9	52
Oklahoma	9		9	327		327	17	6	23
South Carolina	49	7	56	1,776	575	2,351	88	32	120
Tennessee	4	5	9	185	264	449	19	4	23
Texas	98	21	119	2,119	581	2,700	87	83	170
Virginia	16	1	17	550	67	617	29	9	38
West Virginia									
District of Columbia									
Total	271	61	332	7,960	4,665	12,625	448	215	663

* Data not available for 1 school in Greene County.

TABLE 4

Enrollment and Number of Teachers in Public Schools Offering 4 Years of Secondary Work for Negroes in 17 Southern States and the District of Columbia, 1932-33

State	Number of Schools			Enrollment			Number of Teachers		
	Rural	Urban	Total	Rural	Urban	Total	Full Time	Part Time	Total
Alabama	40	11	51	2,700	4,629	7,329	250	72	322
Arkansas	5	13	18	303	2,230	2,533	126	14	140
Delaware		2	2		752	752	20	2	22
Florida	3	29	32	98	4,689	4,787	173	41	214
Georgia	27	27	54	1,948	5,655	7,603	232	38	270
Kentucky	13	36	49	487	3,608	4,095	202	17	219
Louisiana	15	26	41	1,041	4,138	5,179	224	38	262
Maryland	9	16	25	690	3,721	4,411	157	11	168
Mississippi	14	16	30	1,191	2,465	365	132	23	155
Missouri	5	17	22	72	4,611	4,683	197	12	209
North Carolina	80	46	126	9,628	11,130	20,758	664	30	694
Oklahoma	32	23	55	2,379	3,066	5,445	261	48	309
South Carolina	23	24	47	1,568	4,944	6,512	214	15	229
Tennessee	14	25	39	1,172	6,038	7,210	233	31	264
Texas	46	76	122	2,364	15,408	17,772	572	94	666
Virginia	48	14	62	3,463	6,758	10,221	363	46	409
West Virginia	14	15	29	1,558	1,846	3,404	196	20	216
District of Columbia		3	3		4,069	4,069	131		131
Total	388	419	807	30,662	89,757	120,419	4,347	552	4,899

APPENDIX C*

Herein are included tables and lists of counties for the seventeen Southern states included in this investigation and the District of Columbia. The tables contain the following information about each state: number of schools by years of work offered and their rural or urban location; the counties offering 0-years, one, two, three, and four years of public secondary education; the Negro population 15 to 19 years of age residing therein; and the percentage of the Negro population 15 to 19 years of age in the state in each of the counties, grouped according to the number of years of public secondary work offered.

Tables also are included which show the enrollment and number of full-time and part-time teachers found in one, two,

*All data presented in this appendix were collected and compiled by the author. Population data were taken from U. S. Census of 1930.

three, and four-year schools. The rural and urban enrollments are differentiated for the four classes of schools. The number of, and enrollment in, accredited schools is also included.

Herein are lists of counties with letters following the names to indicate the approximate location in the state. The Negro population 15 to 19 years of age in a given county follows its name. Counties are classified as to those providing 0, 1, 2, 3, or 4 years of public secondary facilities for Negroes. Those counties possessing four-year state accredited schools are also indicated. Other information to facilitate interpretation is included.

TABLE 1

PUBLIC SECONDARY SCHOOLS FOR NEGROES IN ALABAMA SHOWN ACCORDING TO NUMBER OF SCHOOLS AND COUNTIES OFFERING 0 TO 4 YEARS OF WORK, 1932-33

Numbers of Years of Work Offered	Number of Schools			Counties Offering		Per Cent of Negro Population of
	Urban	Rural	Total	Number	Population 15 to 19 years of age	State, 15 to 19 years living in Counties Offering
0 years				10	3,807*	3.5
1 year only	11	47	58	10	10,803	9.9
2 years only	13	5	18	4	5,509	5.
3 years only	2	6	8	5	5,215	4.8
4 years	11	40	51	38	83,882	76.8
Total	37	98	135	67	109,216	100.0

* Of this number 2 Negroes constitute the population 15 to 19 years of age in 1 county.

TABLE 2

ENROLLMENT AND NUMBER OF TEACHERS BY YEARS OF WORK OFFERED IN PUBLIC SECONDARY SCHOOLS FOR NEGROES IN ALABAMA, 1932-33

Schools Offering	Enrollment								Number of Teachers		
	Years of Work Offered							In Accredited Schools	Full Time	Part Time	Total
	I	II	III	IV	Total	Urban	Rural				
1 year only	634				634	354	280		17	57	74
2 years only	226	198			424	281	143		12	22	34
3 years only	159	102	88		349	113	236		12	9	21
4 years	2,435	1,924	1,598	1,372	7,329	4,629	2,700	3,285*	250	72	322
Total	3,454	2,224	1,686	1,372	8,736	5,377	3,359	3,285	291	160	451ᵃ

* There are 5 accredited 4-year secondary schools included in this study.
ᵃ Partially estimated.

ALABAMA
(1932-1933)

PUBLIC SECONDARY SCHOOL WORK OFFERED IN COUNTIES

None: (10)

Blount (N)	132	Lauderdale (Nw)	903	Marshall (N)	164
Cherokee (Ne)	223	Limestone (N)	1,207	Washington (Sw)	831
Cleburne (Ne)	89	Marion (Nw)	115	Winston (N)	2
Franklin (Nw)	141				

1 Year Only: (10)

Butler (S)	1,815	Dale (Se)	687	Jackson (Ne)	357
Barbour (Se)	2,396	Geneva (Se)	493	Pike (Se)	1,813
Crenshaw (S)	935	Houston (Se)	1,698	St. Clair (W)	552
Cullman (N)	57				

2 Years Only: (4)

Bullock (Se)	2,131	Lawrence (N)	863	Macon (E)	2,435
De Kalb (Ne)	80				

3 Years Only: (5)

Baldwin (Sw)	768	Greene (W)	1,795	Tallapoosa (E)	1,218
Etowah (Ne)	1,112	Lamar (Nw)	322		

4 Years, but no Accredited School in the County: (34)

Autauga (C)	1,315	Covington (S)	887	Morgan (N)	878
Bibb (C)	757	Dallas (S)	5,060	Perry (C)	2,370
Calhoun (Ne)	1,434	Elmore (C)	1,684	Pickens (W)	1,396
Chambers (E)	2,413	Escambia (S)	1,060	Randolph (E)	733
Chilton (C)	502	Fayette (Nw)	350	Russell (E)	2,464
Choctaw (Sw)	1,359	Henry (Se)	1,407	Shelby (C)	789
Clark (Sw)	1,631	Lee (E)	2,355	Talladega (C)	2,274
Clay (E)	352	Lowndes (S)	2,453	Tuscaloosa (W)	2,442
Coffee (Se)	862	Madison (N)	2,216	Walker (N)	707
Colbert (Nw)	950	Marengo (W)	2,933	Wilcox (S)	2,354
Conecuh (S)	1,362	Monroe (S)	1,913		
Coosa (C)	669	Montgomery (S)	6,305		

Counties Having One or More Accredited 4-Year Secondary Schools: (5)

Hale (W)	2,330	Mobile (Sw)	4,066	Wilcox (S)	2,354
Jefferson (C)	15,940	Sumter* (W)	2,484		

NOTE: De Kalb County (80) has fewest Negroes 15 to 19 years of age for whom any secondary work is offered.

The Negro population 15 to 19 years of age is 11.6 per cent of the total Negro population of the State of Alabama.

* Snow Hill Institute.

TABLE 3

PUBLIC SECONDARY SCHOOLS FOR NEGROES IN ARKANSAS SHOWN ACCORDING TO NUMBER OF SCHOOLS AND COUNTIES OFFERING 0 TO 4 YEARS OF WORK, 1932-33

Number of Years of Work Offered	Number of Schools			Counties Offering		Per Cent of Negro Population of State, 15 to 19 years living in Counties Offering
	Urban	Rural	Total	Number	Population 15 to 19 years of age	
0 years				32	4,813*	9.1
1 year only	5	20	25	9	5,163	9.8
2 years only	8	12	20	15	13,322	25.4
3 years only	3	7	10	6	7,371	14.0
4 years	13	5	18	13	21,876	41.7
Total	29	44	73	75	52,545	100.0

* Of this number, 251 are distributed among 25 counties having less than 50 Negroes 15 to 19 years of age.

TABLE 4

ENROLLMENT AND NUMBER OF TEACHERS BY YEARS OF WORK OFFERED IN PUBLIC SECONDARY SCHOOLS FOR NEGROES IN ARKANSAS, 1932-33

Schools Offering	Enrollment								Number of Teachers		
	Years of Work Offered				Total	Urban	Rural	In Accredited Schools	Full Time	Part Time	Total
	I	II	III	IV							
1 year only..	279				279	62	217		11	27	38
2 years only	229	169			398	209	189		17	17	34
3 years only	196	123	79		398	141	257		14	12	26
4 years	808	713	546	466	2,533	2,230	303	2,403*	126	14	140
Total	1,512	1,005	625	466	3,608	2,642	966	2,403	168	70	238

* There are 15 accredited 4-year secondary schools included in this study.

ARKANSAS
(1932-1933)

PUBLIC SECONDARY SCHOOL WORK OFFERED IN COUNTIES

None: (32)

Baxter (N)	0	Greene (Ne)	1	Pike (Sw)	40
Benton (Nw)	3	Izard (N)	26	Poinsett (Ne)	403
Boone (Nw)	0	Johnson (Nw)	29	Polk (W)	0
Carroll (Nw)	2	Lawrence (Ne)	45	Pope (Nw)	0
Clay (N)	0	Logan (W)	63	Randolph (Ne)	27
Cleburne (N)	0	Madison (Nw)	1	Saline (C)	55
Cleveland (S)	0	Marion (N)	1	Scott (W)	1
Crawford (Nw)	118	Montgomery		Searcy (N)	0
Franklin (Nw)	47	(W)	14	Sharp (N)	1
Fulton (N)	0	Newton (Nw)	0	Stone (N)	1
Grant (C)	108	Perry (C)	40	Van Buren (N)	12

1 Year Only: (9)

Bradley (S)	592	Nevada (Sw)	913	Woodruff (E)	1,283
Faulkner (C)	411	Washington		Yell (W)	124
Lonoke (C)	1,304	(Nw)	59		
Hot Springs (C)	251	White (C)	226		

2 Years Only: (15)

Arkansas (E)	497	Drew (Se)	1,076	Mississippi (Ne)	2,724
Calhoun (S)	380	Independence		Monroe (E)	1,261
Clark (Sw)	933	(N)	101	Prairie (C)	44
Columbia (Sw)	1,540	Jackson (Ne)	596	Sevier (Sw)	232
Crittenden (E)	3,283	Lafayette (Sw)	953		
Cross (E)	1,230	Lincoln (Se)	1,385		

3 Years Only: (6)

Ashley (Se)	1,351	Howard (Sw)	493	St. Francis (E)	2,620
Conway (C)	753	Little River			
Desha (N)	1,378	(Sw)	493		

4 Years, but no Accredited Secondary School in the County: (2)

Craighead*		Dallas* (S)	638
(Ne)	138		

Counties Having one Accredited 4-Year Secondary School, or More (11)

Ashley (Se)	1,351	Jefferson (C)	4,051	Pulaski (C)	3,976
Chicot (Se)	1,418	Lee (E)	1,782	Sebastian (W)	447
Garland (C)	428	Miller (Sw)	975	Union (S)	1,975
Hempstead (Sw)	1,647	Ouachita (S)	1,547		

* One school in each county was accredited by 1934.

Note: Washington County (59) has the fewest Negroes 15 to 19 years of age for whom any secondary work is offered.

Note: The Negro population 15 to 19 years of age is 11.6% of the total Negro population of the State of Arkansas.

TABLE 5

PUBLIC SECONDARY SCHOOLS FOR NEGROES IN DELAWARE SHOWN ACCORDING TO NUMBER OF SCHOOLS AND COUNTIES OFFERING 0 TO 4 YEARS OF WORK, 1932-33

Number of Years of Work Offered	Number of Schools			Counties Offering		
	Urban	Rural	Total	Number	Population 15 to 19 years of age	Per Cent of Negro Population of State, 15 to 19 years living in Counties Offering
0 years						
1 year only		2	2			
2 years only						
3 years only		2	2			
4 years	2		2	3	2,985	100.0
Total	2	4	6	3	2,985	100.0

TABLE 6

ENROLLMENT AND NUMBER OF TEACHERS BY YEARS OF WORK OFFERED IN PUBLIC SECONDARY SCHOOLS FOR NEGROES IN DELAWARE, 1932-33

Schools Offering	Enrollment								Number of Teachers		
	Years of Work Offered				Total	Urban	Rural	In Accredited Schools	Full Time	Part Time	Total
	I	II	III	IV							
1 year only..	24				24		24		2		2
2 years only											
3 years only	32	24	14		70		70		2		2
4 years........	253	211	176	112	752	752		752*	20	2	22
Total	309	235	190	112	846	752	94	275	24	2	26

* There are 2 accredied 4-year secondary schools included in this study.

TABLE 7

PUBLIC SECONDARY SCHOOLS FOR NEGROES IN THE DISTRICT OF COLUMBIA SHOWN ACCORDING TO NUMBER OF SCHOOLS, NUMBER OF TEACHERS, AND ENROLLMENT FOR 1932-33

Number Years of Work Offered	Schools	Enrollment					Number of Teachers		
		Years of Work Offered				Total	Full Time	Part Time	Total
		I	II	III	IV				
1 year only............	5	1,114*				1,114	36[a]		36
2 years only...........									
3 years only...........									
4 years	3	635	1,582	996	856	4,069	131		131
Total	8[b]	1,749	1,582	996	856	5,183[b]	167		167

*Ninth grade enrollment of 5 junior high schools in Washington.
[a] Estimated.
[b] These schools are all located in Washington and are approved or accredited. There are 10,675 Negroes 15 to 19 years of age in the District of Columbia.

TABLE 8

PUBLIC SECONDARY SCHOOLS FOR NEGROES IN FLORIDA SHOWN ACCORDING TO NUMBER OF SCHOOLS AND COUNTIES OFFERING 0 TO 4 YEARS OF WORK, 1932-33

Number of Years of Work Offered	Number of Schools			Counties Offering		Per Cent of Negro Population of State, 15 to 19 years living in Counties Offering
	Urban	Rural	Total	Number	Population 15 to 19 years of age	
0 years				29	6,080	14.0
1 year only	4	9	13	3	1,175	2.7
2 years only	10	3	13	8	3,348	7.7
3 years only	1		1	0		0.0
4 years	29	3	32	27	32,752	75.6
Total	44	15	59	67	43,355	100.0

TABLE 9

ENROLLMENT AND NUMBER OF TEACHERS BY YEARS OF WORK OFFERED IN PUBLIC SECONDARY SCHOOLS FOR NEGROES IN FLORIDA, 1932-33

Schools Offering	Enrollment							In Accredited School	Number of Teachers		
	Years of Work Offered				Total	Urban	Rural		Full Time	Part Time	Total
	I	II	III	IV							
1 year only..	106				106	20	86		5	11	16
2 years only	163	110			273	213	60		14	23	37
3 years only	17	16	7		40	40			2	1	3
4 years	1,666	1,337	1,026	758	4,787	4,689	98	1,858	173	41	214
Total	1,952	1,463	1,033	758	5,206	4,962	244	1,858*	194	76	270[a]

* There are 9 accredited schools included in this study.

[a] Partially estimated due to 6 year high school organization in some systems.

FLORIDA
(1932-1933)
PUBLIC SECONDARY SCHOOL WORK OFFERED IN COUNTIES

None: (28)

Baker (Ne)	167	Gulf (Nw)	110	Liberty (Nw)	140
Bay (Nw)	324	Hamilton (N)	418	Oceola (C)	277
Bradford (Ne)	317	Hardee (Sw)	91	Okaloosa (Nw)	124
Calhoun (Nw)	163	Hendry (S)	128	Okeechobee (Se)	70
Charlotte (Sw)	63	Hernando (W)	163	Pasco (W)	186
Citrus (W)	191	Holmes (Nw)	54	Santa Rosa	
Collier (S)	70	Indian River (E)	213	(Nw)	252
Flagler (E)	73	Jefferson (N)	1,123	Union (Ne)	238
Gilchrist (N)	70	Lafayette (N)	68	Washington	
Glades (S)	91	Levy (W)	458	(Nw)	295

1 Year Only: (3)

Martin (Se) 155   Sumter (C) 348   Suwannee (N) 672

2 Years Only: (8)

Broward (S)	710	Highlands (C)	242	Taylor (N)	451
De Sota (Sw)	143	Madison (N)	1,032	Walton (Nw)	283
Franklin (Nw)	237	Sarasota (Sw)	250		

3 Years Only: (0)

4 Years, but no Accredited School in County: (18)

Brevard (E)	350	Jackson (Nw)	1,734	Pinellas (W)	1,061
Clay (Ne)	160	Lake (C)	659	Putnam (Ne)	792
Columbia (N)	681	Manatee (Sw)	745	St. Johns (Ne)	758
Duval (Ne)	4,879	Marion (C)	1,621	Seminole (C)	971
Gadsden (Nw)	1,992	Monroe (S)	237	Wakulla* (Nw)	257
Hillsborough		Nassau (Ne)	438		
(W)	2,597	Orange (C)	1,212		

Counties Having One Accredited Secondary School, or More: (9)

Alachua (N)	1,730	Leon (Nw)	1,534	St. Lucie (Se)	153
Dade (S)	2,399	Palm Beach		Volusia (E)	1,188
Escambia (Nw)	1,283	(Se)	1,346		
Lee (Sw)	319	Polk (C)	1,552		

* Data referring to this county not verified.
St. Lucie (153) County has the fewest Negroes 15 to 19 years of age for whom any secondary work is offered.
The Negro population 15 to 19 years of age is 10 per cent of the total Negro population of the State of Florida.

TABLE 10

PUBLIC SECONDARY SCHOOLS FOR NEGROES IN GEORGIA SHOWN ACCORDING TO NUMBER OF SCHOOLS AND COUNTIES OFFERING 0 TO 4 YEARS OF WORK, 1932-33

Number of Years of Work Offered	Number of Schools			Counties Offering		Per Cent of Negro Population of State, 15 to 19 years living in Counties Offering
	Urban	Rural	Total	Number	Population 15 to 19 years of age	
0 years				34	11,216*	8.4
1 year only	5	46	51	22	12,348	9.2
2 years only	9	62	71	36	21,921	16.3
3 years only	3	27	30	17	15,130	11.3
4 years	27	27	54	50	73,601	54.8
Total	44	162	206	159	134,216	100.0

TABLE 11

ENROLLMENT AND NUMBER OF TEACHERS BY YEARS OF WORK OFFERED IN PUBLIC SECONDARY SCHOOLS FOR NEGROES IN GEORGIA, 1932-33

Schools Offering	Enrollment								Number of Teachers		
	Years of Work Offered				Total	Urban	Rural	In Accredited Schools	Full Time	Part Time	Total
	I	II	III	IV							
1 year only..	633				633*	374	259		16	45	61
2 years only	865	565			1,430	370	1,060		46	54	100
3 years only	284	236	185		705	165	540		31	17	48
4 years	2,695	1,893	1,685	1,330	7,603	5,655	1,948	3,997ª	232	38	270
Total	4,477	2,694	1,870	1,330	10,371	6,564	3,807	3,997	325	154	479

*Of this number 318 are in the 9th grade of junior high school in Savannah and housed in a separate school.
ª There are 14 accredited 4 year secondary schools included in this study.

Appendix

GEORGIA
(1932-1933)
PUBLIC SECONDARY SCHOOL WORK OFFERED IN COUNTIES

None: (34)

County	#	County	#	County	#
Atkinson (S)	211	Dade (Nw)	19	Lumpkin (N)	26
Bacon (Se)	118	Dawson (N)	11	Madison (Ne)	409
Baker (Sw)	637	Douglas (W)	296	Murray (Nw)	37
Banks (Ne)	137	Echols (S)	96	Quitman (Sw)	354
Bleckley (C)	440	Fannin (N)	3	Rabun (Ne)	24
Brantley (Se)	144	Forsyth (N)	2	Richmond (E)	3,243
Bryan (E)	339	Gilmer (N)	1	Taliferro (Ne)	550
Catoosa (Nw)	66	Glascock (E)	321	Towns (Ne)	0
Charlton (Se)	105	Habersham (Ne)	103	Twiggs (C)	754
Chattahoochie (W)	258	Haralson (Nw)	161	Union (N)	10
Crawford (C)	490	Irwin (S)	693	Wheeler (C)	387
				White (Ne)	49

1 Year Only: (22)

County	#	County	#	County	#
Appling (Se)	345	Jackson (N)	544	Talbot (W)	815
Calhoun (Sw)	1,023	Long (Se)	239	Upson (W)	924
Crisp (C)	1,028	McIntosh (Se)	450	Walker (Nw)	318
Effingham (E)	452	Miller (Sw)	467	Webster (W)	427
Fayette (W)	394	Oconee (Ne)	339	Whitefield (Nw)	164
Gordon (Nw)	154	Paulding (Nw)	150	Wilkinson (C)	690
Harris (W)	975	Pike (W)	736		
Upson (W)	924	Richmond (E)	3,243		

2 Years Only: (36)

County	#	County	#	County	#
Bartow (Nw)	568	Heard (W)	297	Rockdale (N)	336
Berrien (S)	289	Houston (C)	904	Schley (W)	491
Camden (Se)	446	Johnson (C)	675	Stephens (Ne)	284
Candler (E)	437	Jones (C)	721	Sumter (W)	2,310
Cherokee (Nw)	109	Lanier (S)	239	Tattnall (Se)	445
Clay (Sw)	555	Lee (Sw)	805	Treutlen (C)	354
Clinch (S)	317	Lincoln (Ne)	564	Turner (S)	533
Coffee (S)	711	McDuffy (E)	571	Walton (N)	919
Columbia (E)	708	Meriwether (W)	1,526	Warren (E)	978
Early (Sw)	1,370	Mitchell (Sw)	1,587	Wayne (Se)	368
Evans (Se)	332	Montgomery (C)	633	Wilcox (C)	706
Gwinnett (N)	442	Pierce (Se)	405	Liberty (Se)	728

3 Years Only: (17)

County	#	County	#	County	#
Barrow (N)	267	Hancock (C)	1,235	Stewart (W)	1,055
Butts (C)	580	Marion (W)	509	Taylor (W)	696
Chattooga (Nw)	286	Morgan (N)	1,003	Telfair (C)	665
De Kalb (N)	1,543	Pickens (N)	106	Terrill (Sw)	1,679
Franklin (Ne)	378	Putnam (C)	736	Worth (S)	1,262
Hall (N)	428	Spalding (W)	1,089		

4 Years, but no Accredited School in the County: (37)

County	#	County	#	County	#
Baldwin (C)	1,197	Elbert (Ne)	1,024	Polk (Nw)	671
Ben Hill (S)	559	Emanuel (E)	1,262	Pulaski (C)	625
Bibb (C)	3,699	Grady (Sw)	922	Screven (E)	1,450
Burke (E)	2,864	Greene (Ne)	812	Seminole (Sw)	438
Carroll (W)	1,084	Hart (Ne)	568	Thomas (S)	2,054
Chatham (E)	538	Jasper (C)	696	Troup (W)	2,030
Clayton (N)	441	Jefferson (E)	1,628	Toombs (Se)	643
Colquitt (S)	1,083	Jenkins (E)	933	Washington (C)	1,767
Cook (S)	391	Lamar (C)	577	Ware (Se)	873
Coweta (W)	391	Laurens (S)	1,721	Wilkes (Ne)	1,248
Dodge (C)	1,069	Macon (C)	1,507	Tift (S)	598
Dooly (C)	1,361	Monroe (C)	943		
Dougherty (Sw)	1,424	Newton (W)	947		

Counties Having One Accredited Secondary School, or More: (13)

Brooks (S)	1,491	Floyd (Nw)	1,096	Muscogee (W)	2,475
Bulloch (E)	1,452	Fulton (N)	11,311	Peach* (C)	912
Clark (Ne)	1,386	Glynn (Se)	910	Randolph (Sw)	1,557
Cobb (Nw)	845	Henry (N)	1,081		
Decatur (Sw)	1,554	Lowndes (S)	1,713		

* Fort Valley N. & I. does public secondary work for county.

Note: Pickens County (106) has the fewest Negroes 15 to 19 years of age for whom any secondary work is offered. The Negro population 15 to 19 years of age is 12.5 per cent of the total Negro population of Georgia.

Note: Data missing for Oglethorpe County (856).

TABLE 12

PUBLIC SECONDARY SCHOOLS FOR NEGROES IN KENTUCKY SHOWN ACCORDING TO NUMBER OF SCHOOLS AND COUNTIES OFFERING 0 TO 4 YEARS OF WORK, 1932-33

Number of Years of Work Offered	Number of Schools			Counties Offering		Per Cent of Negro Population of State, 15 to 19 years living in Counties Offering
	Urban	Rural	Total	Number	Population 15 to 19 years of age	
0 years				56	1,622*	7.8
1 year only	3	1	4	1	120	.6
2 years only	2	12	14	13	1,600	7.7
3 years only	3	8	11	10	1,463	7.0
4 years	36	13	49	40	15,957	76.9
Total	44	34	78	120	20,762	100.0

* Of this number 793 are distributed among 46 counties having less than 50 Negroes 15 to 19 years of age.

TABLE 13

ENROLLMENT AND NUMBER OF TEACHERS BY YEARS OF WORK OFFERED IN PUBLIC SECONDARY SCHOOLS FOR NEGROES IN KENTUCKY, 1932-33

Schools Offering	Enrollment							Number of Teachers			
	Years of Work Offered				Total	Urban	Rural	In Accredited Schools	Full Time	Part Time	Total
	I	II	III	IV							
1 year only	543	10			543	535*	8		22*	1	23
2 years only	123	97			220	45	175		12	7	19
3 years only	128	58	62		248	60	188		11	9	20
4 years	1,079	1,228	969	819	4,095	3,608	487	3,705a	202	17	219
Total	1,873	1,383	1,031	819	5,106	4,248	858	3,705	247	34	281

* All enrolled in 9th grade of junior high schools in 3 cities. All teaching in 9th grade of junior high schools in 3 cities.

a There are 38 accredited 4 year secondary schools included in this study.

Appendix

KENTUCKY
(1932-1933)
PUBLIC SECONDARY SCHOOL WORK OFFERED IN COUNTIES

None: (56)

County	#	County	#	County	#
Allen (S)	49	Grant (N)	13	Martin (E)	0
Bath (Ne)	81	Grayson (W)	12	Meade (Nw)	37
Bracken (E)	22	Green (C)	104	Menifee (E)	7
Breathitt (E)	17	Greenup (Ne)	21	Metcalf (S)	48
Butler (W)	28	Hancock (Nw)	30	Monroe (S)	61
Carlisle (Sw)	36	Jackson (Se)	4	Morgan (E)	4
Campbell (N)	105	Johnson (E)	7	Owsley (Se)	5
Carroll (N)	41	Knott (Se)	26	Pendleton (N)	10
Carter (Ne)	7	Larue (C)	60	Powell (E)	22
Casey (C)	11	Lawrence (Ne)	17	Robertson (N)	6
Clinton (Se)	2	Lee (E)	8	Rockcastle (Se)	10
Crittenden (W)	31	Leslie (Se)	3	Rowan (Ne)	3
Cumberland (S)	80	Lewis (Ne)	3	Russell (S)	23
Edmonson (W)	22	Livingston (W)	34	Spencer (C)	53
Elliott (Ne)	0	Lyon (Sw)	108	Taylor (C)	113
Estill (E)	15	McCreary (S)	3	Trimble (N)	0
Fleming (Ne)	57	McLean (W)	44	Whitley (Se)	35
Floyd (E)	60	Magoffin (E)	3	Wolfe (E)	1
Gallatin (N)	17	Marshall (Sw)	6		

1 Year Only: (1)

County	#
Pike (E)	120

2 Years Only: (13)

County	#	County	#	County	#
Ballard (Sw)	121	Hart (C)	140	Oldham (N)	72
Boone (N)	30	Henry (N)	119	Wayne (S)	65
Bullitt (C)	37	Hickman (Sw)	109	Marion (C)	159
Fulton (Sw)	372	Lincoln (C)	205		
Garrard (C)	124	Nicholas (N)	49		

3 Years Only: (10)

County	#	County	#	County	#
Anderson (C)	53	Letcher (Se)	171	Union (W)	184
Barren (S)	310	Ohio (W)	66	Washington (C)	145
Clay (Se)	31	Owen (N)	64		
Harrison (N)	84	Todd (Sw)	355		

4 Years, but no Accredited School in County: (7)

County	#	County	#	County	#
Adair (S)	124	Harlan (Se)	478	Mercer (C)	129
Breckenridge (Nw)	126	Knox (Se)	74	Simpson (S)	198
		Laurel (Se)	37		

Counties Having One Accredited Secondary School, or More: (33)

County	#	County	#	County	#
Bell (Se)	201	Hardin (Ne)	143	Muhlenberg (W)	310
Bourbon (N)	330	Henderson (Nw)	433	Nelson (C)	196
Boyd (Ne)	86	Hopkins (W)	516	Perry (Se)	228
Boyle (C)	325	Jefferson (N)	3,890	Pulaski (S)	99
Caldwell (W)	177	Jessamine (C)	172	Scott (N)	211
Calloway (Sw)	107	Kenton (N)	277	Trigg (Sw)	244
Christian (Sw)	1,244	Logan (Sw)	367	Warren (S)	562
Clark (C)	244	McCracken (Sw)	707	Webster (W)	293
Daviess (Nw)	330	Madison (C)	464	Woodford (C)	216
Fayette (C)	1,401	Mason (Ne)	213	Shelby (N)	212
Franklin (Ne)	211	Montgomery (Ne)	173		
Graves (Sw)	232				

Note: Boone County (30) has the fewest Negroes 15 to 19 years of age for whom any secondary work is offered. Two years of work are offered. Those who go beyond the second year are transported to Covington.

Note: The Negro population 15 to 19 years of age is 9.2 per cent of the total Negro population of the State of Kentucky.

TABLE 14

Public Secondary Schools for Negroes in Louisiana Shown According to Number of Schools and Counties Offering 0 to 4 Years of Work, 1932-33

Number of Years of Work Offered	Number of Schools			Counties Offering		Per Cent of Negro Population of State, 15 to 19 years living in Counties Offering
	Urban	Rural	Total	Number	Population 15 to 19 years of age	
0 years				18	12,814	15.8
1 year only	2	4	6	2	1,648	2.0
2 years only	2	7	9	2	831	1.0
3 years only	5	6	11	4	1,704	2.1
4 years	26	15	41	38	64,296	79.1
Total	35	32	67	64	81,293	100.0

TABLE 15

Enrollment and Number of Teachers by Years of Work Offered in Public Secondary Schools for Negroes in Louisiana, 1932-33

Schools Offering	Enrollment								Number of Teachers		
	Years of Work Offered				Total	Urban	Rural	In Accredited Schools	Full Time	Part Time	Total
	I	II	III	IV							
1 year only	66				66	21	45		3	4	7
2 years only	82	61			143	39	104		9	6	15
3 years only	1,148	747	236		2,131	1,998	133		57	10	67
4 years	1,626	1,234	1,122	1,197	5,179	4,138	1,041	4,459*	224	38	262
Total	2,922	2,042	1,358	1,197	7,519	6,196	1,323	4,459	293	58	351

* There are 3 accredited schools included in this study. The 2 junior high schools and the one senior high school in New Orleans were grouped as one accredited unit. There are 37 other schools approved by the State on a lower level than the accredited schools.

Appendix

LOUISIANA
(1932-1933)
PUBLIC SECONDARY SCHOOL WORK OFFERED IN PARISHES

None: (18)

Avoyelles (C)....	1,124	Jefferson Davis (Sw)	534	St. Charles (Se)	400
Baton Rouge (W)	572	Lafourche (Se)..	527	St. James (Se)..	793
Cameron (Sw)....	70	Livingston (Se)	470	St. Martin (S)..	965
Evangeline (C)..	711	Pointe Coupee (C)	1,324	Terrebonne (Se)	886
East Feliciana (E)	1,316	Red River (Nw)	796	Vermilion (S)....	553
West Feliciana (C)	927	St. Bernard (Se)	136	St. John (Se)....	700

1 Year Only: (2)

Assumption (Se)	612	East Carroll (Ne)	1,036

2 Years Only: (2)

W. Carroll (Ne)	308	Plaquemines (Se)	538

3 Years Only: (4)

Ascension (Se)..	694	Jackson (N)......	495
Caldwell (Ne)....	325	LaSalle (C)........	190

4 Years, But No Accredited Seconday School:* (35)

Acadia (S)........	1,042	Iberia (S)..........	1,254	St. Landry (S)..	3,620
Allen (Sw)........	374	Iberville (Se)....	1,162	St. Mary (S)......	1,502
Beauregard (Sw)..............	330	Jefferson (Se)....	691	St. Tammany (S)	789
		Lafayette (S)....	1,643		
Bienville (Nw)..	1,296	Lincoln (N)......	1,065	Tangipahoa (E)	1,863
Bossier (Nw)....	1,843	Madison (Ne)....	902	Tensas (Ne)........	1,022
Calcasieu (Sw)..	1,344	Morehouse (Ne)	1,471	Union (N)..........	751
Catahoula (C)....	490	Natchitoches (C)	257	Vernon (W)........	347
Claiborne (N)....	2,170	Ouachita (N)	1,862	Washington (E)	1,075
Concordia (C)....	875	Rapides (C)........	2,656	Webster (Nw)....	1,609
DeSota (Nw)....	1,119	Richland (Ne)....	1,438	Winn (C)............	350
Franklin (Ne)....	1,201	Sabine (W)........	565		
Grant (C)..........	520	St. Helena (E)..	569		

Parish Has One Secondary School Accredited, or More: (3)

E. Baton Rouge (Se)	3,122	Caddo (Nw)........	5,875
		Orleans (Se)......11,340	

* According to Mr. A. C. Lewis, State Agent for Negro Schools, these schools are state approved on a little lower level than accredited schools.

Note: LaSalle Parish (190) has the fewest Negroes 15 to 19 years of age for whom any secondary work is offered.

Note: The Negro population 15 to 19 years of age is 10.5 per cent of the total Negro population of the State of Louisiana.

TABLE 16

Public Secondary Schools for Negroes in Maryland Shown According to Number of Schools and Counties Offering 0 to 4 Years of Work, 1932-33

Number of Years of Work Offered	Number of Schools			Counties Offering		Per Cent of Negro Population of State, 15 to 19 years living in Counties Offering
	Urban	Rural	Total	Number	Population 15 to 19 years of age	
0 years				3**	1,005*	3.9
1 year only	3		3	0		.0
2 years only	1	2	3	0		.0
3 years only				0		.0
4 years	16	9	25	20	24,412	96.1
Total	20	11	31	23	25,417	100.0

** These counties are Garrett, Howard and St. Mary's.
* Of this number, 3 Negroes constitute the population 15 to 19 years of age in 1 county.

TABLE 17

Enrollment and Number of Teachers by Years of Work Offered in Public Secondary Schools for Negroes in Maryland, 1932-33

Schools Offering	Enrollment							In Accredited Schools	Number of Teachers		
	Years of Work Offered				Total	Urban	Rural		Full Time	Part Time	Total
	I	II	III	IV							
1 year only	731				731	731†			24†		24
2 years only	66	40			106	33	73		3	1	4
3 years only											
4 years	1,332	1,336	978	765	4,411	3,721	690	4,111*	157	11	168
Total	2,129	1,376	978	765	5,248	4,485	763	4,411	184	12	196

† All located in 9th grade of 3 junior high schools in Baltimore.
* There are 25 approved or accredited 4 year secondary schools included in this study. Graduates are admitted to higher institutions without examinaion.

TABLE 18

PUBLIC SECONDARY SCHOOLS FOR NEGROES IN MISSISSIPPI SHOWN ACCORDING TO NUMBER OF SCHOOLS AND COUNTIES OFFERING 0 TO 4 YEARS OF WORK, 1932-33

Number of Years of Work Offered	Number of Schools			Counties Offering		Per Cent of Negro Population of State, 15 to 19 years living in Counties Offering
	Urban	Rural	Total	Number	Population 15 to 19 years of age	
0 years				16	15,955	13.9
1 year only	3	30	33	10	7,062	6.1
2 years only	4	43	47	21	21,094	18.4
3 years only	7	11	18	9	13,902	12.1
4 years	16	14	30	26	56,880	49.5
Total	30	98	128	82	114,893	100.0

TABLE 19

ENROLLMENT AND NUMBER OF TEACHERS BY YEARS OF WORK OFFERED IN PUBLIC SECONDARY SCHOOLS FOR NEGROES IN MISSISSIPPI, 1932-33

Schools Offering	Enrollment							In Accredited Schools	Number of Teachers		
	Years of Work Offered				Total	Urban	Rural		Full Time	Part Time	Total
	I	II	III	IV							
1 year only..	337				337	74	263		12	21	33
2 years only	656	504			1,160	116	1,044		49	39	88
3 years only	364	241	220		825	410	415		31	14	45
4 years	1,246	1,018	806	586	3,656	2,465	1,191	156*	132	23	155
Total	2,603	1,763	1,026	586	5,978	3,065	2,913	156	224	97	321

* There is only one accredited 4 year secondary school included in this study. The State Supervisor of Negro Education, Mr. P. H. Easom, has approved 23 schools for 4 years' work but they have not met the State standards as yet.

MISSISSIPPI
(1932-1933)
PUBLIC SECONDARY SCHOOL WORK OFFERED IN COUNTIES

None: (15)

Benton (N)	564	Kemper (E)	1,569	Tishomingo	
Calhoun (N)	362	Marshall (N)	2,212	(Ne)	101
Choctaw (C)	436	Pontotoc (N)	499	Tunica (Nw)	1,837
De Sota (Nw)	224	Rankin (C)	1,391	Wayne (Se)	643
Itawamba (Ne)	132	Tate (Nw)	1,294	Wilkinson (Sw)	1,080
Jasper (E)	1,116				

1 Year Only: (10)

Clay (E)	1,389	Quitman (Nw)	1,842	Webster (C)	318
George (Se)	140	Simpson (S)	804	Yalobusha (N)	949
Issaquena (W)	464	Smith (C)	454		
Perry (Se)	311	Tippah (N)	391		

2 Years Only: (21)

Claiborne (Sw)	1,068	Jackson (Se)	394	Newton (E)	984
Clarke (E)	968	Jefferson (Sw)	1,279	Pearl River (S)	524
Copiah (Sw)	1,916	Lamar (S)	267	Panola (Nw)	2,102
Covington (S)	548	Lawrence (S)	610	Scott (C)	1,016
Greene (Se)	268	Montgomery (C)	786	Sharkey (W)	1,118
Granada (N)	1,201	Noxubee (E)	2,362	Stone (Se)	154
Humphreys (W)	1,911	Neshoba (W)	655	Winston (E)	962

3 Years Only: (9)

Amity (Sw)	1,259	Hancock (S)	315	Prentiss (Ne)	311
Attala (C)	1,326	Lowndes (E)	2,122	Sunflower (W)	5,345
Carroll (C)	1,492	Marion (S)	960	Walthall (S)	783

4 Years, But No Accredited Secondary School: (24)

Alcorn (Ne)	466	Jones* (Se)	0	Tallahatchie*	
Bolivar* (W)	5,452	Lafayette* (N)	1,022	(Nw)	2,714
Chickasaw (N)	1,323	Lauderdale* (E)	2,433	Union* (N)	659
Coahoma* (Nw)	4,048	Leake* (C)	906	Washington*	
Forest* (Se)	1,009	Lee* (Ne)	4,574	(W)	3,713
Harrison* (Se)	1,013	Lincoln (Sw)	1,009	Yazoo* (W)	659
Hinds* (W)	5,099	Madison (C)	3,360		
Holmes* (C)	3,269	Monroe* (Ne)	1,791		
Jefferson Davis		Oktibbeha* (E)	1,402		
(S)	1,029	Pike* (Sw)	1,760		

County Has One Accredited 4-Year Secondary School, or More: (2)

Adams (Sw) 1,616   Warren (W) 1,954

* Approved by Mr. P. Easom, State Agent of Negro Education.

Note: George County (140) has the fewest Negroes 15 to 19 years of age for whom any secondary work is offered.

Note: The Negro population 15 to 19 years of age is 11.4 per cent of the total population of the state of Mississippi.

TABLE 20

PUBLIC SECONDARY SCHOOLS FOR NEGROES IN MISSOURI SHOWN ACCORDING TO NUMBER OF SCHOOLS AND COUNTIES OFFERING 0 TO 4 YEARS OF WORK, 1932-33

Number of Years of Work Offered	Number of Schools			Counties Offering		Per Cent of Negro Population of State, 15 to 19 years living in Counties Offering
	Urban	Rural	Total	Number	Population 15 to 19 years of age	
0 years				82	1,451*	8.2
1 year only		1	1	0		0.0
2 years only	8	2	10	8	681	3.2
3 years only	1	2	3	3	1,714	9.7
4 years	17	5	22	21	13,889	78.9
Total	26	10	36	114	17,735	100.0

* Of this number 683 are distributed among 72 counties having less than 50 Negroes 15 to 19 years of age.

TABLE 21

ENROLLMENT AND NUMBER OF TEACHERS BY YEARS OF WORK OFFERED IN PUBLIC SECONDARY SCHOOLS FOR NEGROES IN MISSOURI, 1932-33

Schools Offering	Enrollment							Number of Teachers		
	Years of Work Offered				Total	Urban	Rural	In Accredited Schools	Full Time	Part Time	Total
	I	II	III	IV							
1 year only	10				10		10		1		1
2 years only	66	54			120	92	28		8	5	13
3 years only	40	32	24		96	16	80		5		5
4 years	1,818	1,245	904	716	4,683	4,611	72	4,595*	197	12	209
Total	1,934	1,331	928	716	4,909	4,719	190	4,595	211	17	228

* There are 14 accredited 4 year schools included in this study.

MISSOURI
(1932-1933)
PUBLIC SECONDARY SCHOOL WORK OFFERED IN COUNTIES

None: (82)

County	#	County	#	County	#
Adair (N)	14	Grundy (N)	1	Polk (S)	4
Andrew (Nw)	2	Harrison (Nw)	0	Pulaski (C)	0
Atchison (Nw)	0	Hickory (C)	0	Putnam (N)	0
Barry (Sw)	0	Holt (Nw)	0	Ralls (Ne)	46
Barton (Sw)	1	Howell (S)	13	Reynolds (Se)	0
Bates (W)	13	Iron (Se)	17	Ripley (Se)	0
Benton (C)	10	Jefferson (E)	106	St. Clair (W)	14
Bollinger (Se)	1	Knox (Ne)	7	Ste. Genevieve (E)	40
Caldwell (Nw)	8	Laclede (S)	22	St. Francois (E)	20
Camden (C)	3	Lawrence (Sw)	9	Schuyler (N)	0
Carter (Se)	0	Lewis (Ne)	47	Scotland (Ne)	0
Cass (W)	19	Lincoln (E)	81	Shelby (Ne)	36
Cedar (W)	0	Linn (N)	37	Stoddard (Se)	237
Christian (S)	1	McDonald (Sw)	0	Stone (S)	0
Clark (Ne)	0	Madison (Se)	20	Sullivan (N)	1
Clinton (Nw)	43	Maries (C)	0	Taney (S)	1
Crawford (E)	0	Mercer (N)	1	Texas (S)	0
Dade (Sw)	4	Miller (C)	10	Vernon (W)	2
Dallas (S)	0	Moniteau (C)	80	Warren (E)	29
Daviess (Nw)	9	Morgan (C)	17	Washington (E)	30
DeKalb (Nw)	2	Newton (Sw)	20	Wayne (Se)	0
Dent (S)	0	Nodaway (Nw)	6	Webster (S)	4
Douglas (S)	0	Oregon (S)	0	Worth (Nw)	0
Dunklin (Se)	51	Osage (C)	7	Wright (S)	14
Franklin (E)	65	Ozark (S)	0	Scott (Se)	151
Gasconade (E)	7	Perry (E)	10	Shannon (S)	0
Gallaway (C)	234	Phelps (C)	10		
Gentry (Nw)	0	Platt (Nw)	29		

1 Year Only: (0)

2 Years Only: (8)

County	#	County	#	County	#
Carroll (N)	45	Johnson (W)	72	Monroe (Ne)	59
Henry (W)	48	Livingston (N)	21	Saline (C)	218
Howard (C)	172	Macon (N)	51		

3 Years Only: (3)

County	#	County	#
New Madrid (Se)	633	Pemiscot (Se)	1,013
		Ray (Nw)	68

4 Years, But No Accredited Secondary School: (8)

County	#	County	#	County	#
Audrain* (Ne)	179	Jasper (Sw)	83	Pike (Ne)	207
Clay (Nw)	84	Lafayette (W)	129	St. Charles (E)	93
Cooper (C)	274	Montgomery*	80		

Counties Having Accredited Four-Year Secondary Schools: (13)

County	#	County	#	County	#
Boone (C)	301	Cole (C)	150	Randolph (N)	186
Buchanan (Nw)	327	Greene (S)	169	St. Louis (E)	849
Butler (Se)	162	Jackson (W)	2,577	St. Louis City (E)	6,683
Cape Girardeau (Se)	134	Marion (Ne)	174		
Chariton (N)	167	Pettis (C)	221		
		Mississippi (Se)	441		

* Data incomplete.

Note: Livingston county (21) has the fewest Negroes 15 to 19 years of age for whom any secondary work is offered.

Note: The Negro population 15 to 19 years of age is 7.9 per cent of the total Negro population of the state of Missouri.

TABLE 22

PUBLIC SECONDARY SCHOOLS FOR NEGROES IN NORTH CAROLINA SHOWN ACCORDING TO NUMBER OF SCHOOLS AND COUNTIES OFFERING 0 TO 4 YEARS OF WORK, 1932-33

Number of Years of Work Offered	Number of Schools			Counties Offering		
	Urban	Rural	Total	Number	Population 15 to 19 years of age	Per Cent of Negro Population of State, 15 to 19 years living in Counties Offering
0 years				12	611*	.5
1 year only	2	13	15	3	573	.5
2 years only	1	31	32	4	632	.5
3 years only	2	26	28	6	1,518	1.3
4 years	46	80	126	75	111,832	97.2
Total	51	150	201	100	115,166	100.0

* Of this number 236 are distributed among 10 counties having less than 50 Negroes 15 to 19 years of age.

TABLE 23

ENROLLMENT AND NUMBER OF TEACHERS BY YEARS OF WORK OFFERED IN PUBLIC SECONDARY SCHOOLS FOR NEGROES IN NORTH CAROLINA, 1932-33

Schools Offering	Enrollment								Number of Teachers		
	Years of Work Offered							In Accredited Schools	Full Time	Part Time	Total
	I	II	III	IV	Total	Urban	Rural				
1 year only..	160				160	25	135		5	12	17
2 years only	492	316			808	164	644		32	6	38
3 years only	608	418	293		1,319	235	1,084		43	9	52
4 years	7,883	5,361	4,145	3,369	20,758	11,130	9,628	18,879*	664	30	694
Total	9,143	6,095	4,438	3,369	23,045	11,554	11,491	18,879	744	57	801

* There are 99 accredited 4 year secondary schools included in this study.

NORTH CAROLINA
(1932-1933)
PUBLIC SECONDARY SCHOOL WORK OFFERED IN COUNTIES

None: (12)

Alleghany (Nw)	26	Clay (Sw)	20	Swain (W)	30
Ashe (Nw)	43	Graham (Sw)	0	Watauga (Nw)	22
Camden (Ne)	254	Madison (W)	34	Yadkin (Nw)	121
Cherokee (Sw)	24	Mitchell (W)	4	Yancey (W)	23

1 Year Only: (3)

McDowell (W)	225	Macon (Sw)	53	Surry (Nw)	295

2 Years Only: (4)

Alexander (Nw)	147	Transylvania		Stokes (N)	332
Jackson (Sw)	80	(Sw)	73		

3 Years Only: (6)

Avery (W)	30	Haywood (W)	88	Pamlico (Se)	393
Dare (E)	49	Henderson (Sw)	250	Rutherford (Sw)	701

4 Years, But Having No Accredited Secondary School in County: (10)

Caldwell (Nw)	278	Hoke (S)	1,248	Scotland (S)	1,476
Caswell (N)	1,089	Hyde (E)	480	Vance (N)	1,543
Davie (C)	311	Lincoln (Sw)	458		
Granville (N)	1,870	Polk (Sw)	217		

The Remaining 65 Counties Have One or More Accredited 4-Year Secondary Schools

Note: Currituck County (271) has the fewest Negroes 15 to 19 years of age for whom a four-year accredited school is available.

Note: Avery County (30) has the fewest Negroes 15 to 19 years of age for whom any secondary work is offered.

Note: The Negro population 15 to 19 years of age is 12.5 per cent of the total Negro population of the state of North Carolina.

TABLE 24

PUBLIC SECONDARY SCHOOLS FOR NEGROES IN OKLAHOMA SHOWN ACCORDING TO NUMBER OF SCHOOLS AND COUNTIES OFFERING 0 TO 4 YEARS OF WORK, 1932-33

Number of Years of Work Offered	Number of Schools			Counties Offering		Per Cent of Negro Population of State, 15 to 19 years living in Counties Offering
	Urban	Rural	Total	Number	Population 15 to 19 years of age	
0 years				39	1,606*	8.5
1 year only	0	1	1	0		0.0
2 years only	1	6	7	3	1,063	5.7
3 years only	0	9	9	1	121	.6
4 years	23	32	55	34	16,021	85.2
Total	24	48	72	77	18,811	100.0

* Of this number 358 are distributed among 27 counties having less than 50 Negroes 15 to 19 years of age.

TABLE 25

ENROLLMENT AND NUMBER OF TEACHERS BY YEARS OF WORK OFFERED IN PUBLIC SECONDARY SCHOOLS FOR NEGROES IN OKLAHOMA, 1932-33

Schools Offering	Enrollment							Number of Teachers		
	Years of Work Offered				Total	Urban	Rural	In Accredited Schools	Full Time	Part Time	Total
	I	II	III	IV							
1 year only	12				12	0	12			1	1
2 years only	55	51			106	12	94		10	3	13
3 years only	138	82	107		327	0	327		17	6	23
4 years	1,800	1,483	1,168	994	5,445	3,066	2,379	3,066*	261	48	309
Total	2,005	1,616	1,275	994	5,890	3,068	2,812	3,066	288	58	346

* There are 25 accredited 4 year secondary schools included in this study.

OKLAHOMA
1932-1933
PUBLIC SECONDARY SCHOOL WORK OFFERED IN COUNTIES

None: (39)

Adair (E)	0	Greer (Sw)	157	Murray (S)	28
Alfalfa (Nw)	1	Harmon (Sw)	57	Ottawa (Ne)	0
Beaver (Nw)	0	Harper (Nw)	0	Pawnee* (N)	90
Beckham (W)	49	Haskell (E)	22	Pontotoc (C)	100
Cherokee (E)	61	Jefferson (S)	18	Pushmataha (C)	37
Cimarron (Nw)	0	Johnson (S)	48	Roger Mills (W)	10
Cleveland (C)	38	Kiowa (Sw)	148	Sequoyah* (E)	182
Coal (S)	64	Latimer (E)	35	Stephens* (S)	40
Cotton (Sw)	19	Love (S)	62	Texas (Nw)	0
Delaware (Ne)	0	Major (Nw)	5	Washita (W)	25
Dewey (W)	2	Marshall (S)	18	Woods (Nw)	0
Ellis (Nw)	0	Mayes (Ne)	58	Woodward (Nw)	0
Grant (N)	2	McClain (C)	64	Le Flore* (E)	205

1 Year Only: (0)

2 Years Only: (3)

Garvine (C)	148	Osage (N)	102	Wagner (Ne)	813

3 Years Only: (1)

Atoka (S) 121

4 Years, But No Accredited Secondary School: (16)

Blain (C)	274	Hughes (C)	241	Pottawatomee (C)	223
Bryan (S)	145	Jackson (Sw)	196	Rodgers (Ne)	81
Caddo (C)	210	Kay (N)	74	Tillman (Sw)	303
Choctaw (Se)	596	McCurtain (Se)	913	Washington (Ne)	96
Craig (Ne)	83	McIntosh (E)	543		
Custer (W)	79	Noble (N)	77		

Counties Having One Accredited Secondary School, or More: (18)

Canadian (C)	95	Kingfisher (C)	210	Okmulgee (E)	1,275
Carter (S)	425	Lincoln (C)	420	Oklahoma (C)	1,643
Comanche (Sw)	132	Logan (C)	830	Payne (C)	194
Creek (C)	845	Muscogee (E)	1,970	Pittsburg (E)	312
Garfield (N)	90	Nowata (Ne)	225	Seminole (C)	662
Grady (C)	259	Okfuskee (C)	999	Tulsa (Ne)	1,428

* It is possible that these counties offer a small amount of unaccredited work in one or more small schools. Accurate data was not available.

Note: Kay county (74) has the fewest Negroes 15 to 19 years of age for whom any secondary work is offered.

Note: The Negro population 15 to 19 years of age is 10.9 per cent of the total population of the state of Oklahoma.

TABLE 26

PUBLIC SECONDARY SCHOOLS FOR NEGROES IN SOUTH CAROLINA SHOWN ACCORDING TO NUMBER OF SCHOOLS AND COUNTIES OFFERING 0 TO 4 YEARS OF WORK, 1932-33

Number of Years of Work Offered	Number of Schools			Counties Offering		Per Cent of Negro Population of State, 15 to 19 years living in Counties Offering
	Urban	Rural	Total	Number	Population 15 to 19 years of age	
0 years						
1 year only	1	81	82	1	898	.8
2 years only	5	51	56	3	5,326	5.0
3 years only	7	49	56	11	20,292	19.0
4 years	24	23	47	31	79,913	75.2
Total	37	204	241	46	106,429	100.0

TABLE 27

ENROLLMENT AND NUMBER OF TEACHERS BY YEARS OF WORK OFFERED IN PUBLIC SECONDARY SCHOOLS FOR NEGROES IN SOUTH CAROLINA, 1932-33

Schools Offering	Enrollment								Number of Teachers		
	Years of Work Offered				Total	Urban	Rural	In Accredited Schools	Full Time	Part Time	Total
	I	II	III	IV							
1 year only..	710				710	24	686		11	75	86
2 years only	551	445			996	186	810		27	49	76
3 years only	996	733	622		2,351	575	1,776		88	32	120
4 years	2,319	1,634	1,353	1,206	6,512	4,944	1,568	1,148*	214	15	229
Total	4,576	2,812	1,975	1,206	10,569	5,729	4,840	1,148	340	171	511

* There are 3 accredited 4 year secondary schools included in this study.

SOUTH CAROLINA
(1932-1933)
PUBLIC SECONDARY SCHOOL WORK OFFERED IN COUNTIES

None: (0)

1 Year Only: (1)

    Jasper (S) 898

2 Years Only: (3)

Chesterfield (Ne) 1,777	Fairfield (N) 2,211	
	Hampton (S) 1,338	

3 Years Only: (11)

Bamberg (Sw).. 1,557	Colleton (S) 1,858	McCormick (W) 1,005
Berkely (Sw) 1,867	Edgefield (W).... 1,661	Pickens (Nw).... 671
Calhoun (C) 1,655	Lee (Ne) 2,319	Williamsburg
Clarendon (C).... 3,186	Lexington (C).... 1,457	(Se) 3,056

4 Years, But No Accredited School in County: (28)

Abbeville (W).... 1,608	Florence (E) 3,724	Newberry (Nw) 2,206
Aiken (W) 2,922	Georgetown (Se) 1,744	Oconee (Nw) 830
Allendale (Sw).. 1,272	Greenville (Nw) 3,593	Orangeburg (C) 5,615
Anderson (Nw).. 3,054	Greenwood (W.. 2,212	Saluda (W) 1,253
Barnwell (Sw).... 1,717	Horry (E) 1,282	Spartanburg
Beaufort (S) 1,887	Kershaw (N) 2,411	(Nw) 4,088
Charleston (Se).. 6,035	Lancaster (N).... 1,610	Sumter (C) 4,168
Chester (N) 2,328	Laurens (Nw).... 2,438	Williamsburg
Dillon (Ne) 1,619	Marion (E) 2,024	(Se) 3,056
Dorchester (Se) 1,605	Marlboro (Ne).. 2,539	York (N) 3,114

Counties Having One Accredited Secondary School, or More: (3)

    Darlington (Ne) 3,063   Union (Nw) 1,791   Richland (C) 4,808

    Note: Pickens (671) has the fewest Negroes 15 to 19 years of age for whom any secondary work is offered.
    Note: The Negro population 15 to 19 years of age is 13.3 per cent of the total Negro population for the State of South Carolina.

TABLE 28

PUBLIC SECONDARY SCHOOLS FOR NEGROES IN TENNESSEE SHOWN ACCORDING TO NUMBER OF SCHOOLS AND COUNTIES OFFERING 0 TO 4 YEARS OF WORK, 1932-33

Number of Years of Work Offered	Number of Schools			Counties Offering		Per Cent of Negro Population of State, 15 to 19 years living in Counties Offering
	Urban	Rural	Total	Number	Population 15 to 19 years of age	
0 years				40	2,415*	4.7
1 year only		1	1	1	203	.4
2 years only	10	16	26	14	2,164	4.2
3 years only	5	4	9	5	1,966	3.8
4 years	25	14	39	35	45,087	86.9
Total	40	35	75	95	51,835	100.0

TABLE 29

ENROLLMENT AND NUMBER OF TEACHERS BY YEARS OF WORK OFFERED IN PUBLIC SECONDARY SCHOOLS FOR NEGROES IN TENNESSEE, 1932-33

Schools Offering	Enrollment							In Accredited Schools	Number of Teachers		
	Years of Work Offered										
	I	II	III	IV	Total	Urban	Rural		Full Time	Part Time	Total
1 year only..	21				21	0	21		1	1	2
2 years only	596	383			979	540	439		29	24	53
3 years only	168	146	135		449	264	185		19	4	23
4 years	2,038	2,153	1,664	1,355	7,210	6,038	1,172	3,668*	233	31	264
Total	2,823	2,682	1,779	1,355	8,659	6,842	1,817	3,668	282	60	342

* There are 28 accredited 4-year schools included in this study.

TENNESSEE
(1932-1933)
PUBLIC SECONDARY SCHOOL WORK OFFERED IN COUNTIES

None: (40)

Anderson (Ne)..	49	Hawkins (Ne)..	117	Perry (W)	25
Benton (Nw)	30	Hancock (Ne)....	17	Pickett (N)	1
Bledsoe (C)	298	Houston (Nw)....	56	Polk (Se)	17
Cannon (C)	32	Humphreys (Nw)	65	Putnam (N)	51
Carter (Ne)	49	Jackson (N)	30	Scott (N)	2
Cheatham (N)....	88	Johnson (Ne)....	34	Sequatchie (S)..	0
Chester (Sw)	234	Lake (N)	487	Sevier (E)	28
Clayborne (Ne)..	78	Lawrence	85	Stewart (Nw)	77
Clay (N)	26	Lewis (C)	52	Unicoi (Ne)	0
Cumberland (C)	9	Macon (N)	43	Union (Ne)	0
DeKalb (C)	59	Meigs (E)	50	Van Buren (C)..	13
Fentress (N)	24	Moore (S)	46	Wayne (S)	55
Grainger (Ne)....	37	Morgan (N)	23		
Grundy (S)	14	Overton (N)	14		

1 Year Only: (1)
McNairy (Sw).... 203

2 Years Only: (14)

Campbell (Ne)....	73	Hickman (C)	138	Smith (N)	150
Coffee (C)	125	Loudon (E)	96	Trousdale (N)..	163
Dixon (N)	234	Marshall (S)	276	Weakley (Nw)..	289
Greene (Ne)	145	Monroe (Se)	127	White (C)	88
Hardin (Sw)	183	Rhea (E)	87		

3 Years Only: (5)

Blount (E)	275	Obion (Nw)	449	Wilson (N)	551
Lincoln (S)	524	Roane (E)	167		

4 Years, But No Accredited School in County: (9)

Crockett (W)	400	Giles (S)	962	Knox (E)	1,857
Decatur (W)	107	Hamblen (Ne)*..	236	Robertson (N)....	641
Franklin (S)	280	Henderson (W)..	958	Sullivan (Ne)....	202

Counties Having One Accredited Four-Year Secondary School, or More: (26)

Bedford (C)	425	Haywood (W)	2,216	Rutherford (C)..	944
Bradley (Se)	209	Henry (Nw)	632	Shelby (Sw)	11,777
Carroll (Nw)	564	Jefferson (E)	174	Sumner (N)	454
Cocke (Ne)	84	Lauderdale (W)	1,190	Tipton (W)	199
Davidson (N)....	5,109	McMinn (Se)	204	Warren (C)	150
Dyer (Nw)	675	Madison (W)....	2,199	Washington (Ne)	272
Fayette (Sw)	2,766	Maury (C)	979		
Gibson (Nw)	1,203	Marion (S)	187	Williamson (C)..	26
Hamilton (Se)....	3,454	Montgomery (N)	1,177		
Hardeman (Sw)	1,012				

* Private School doing some public secondary work.

Notes: Campbell County (73) has the fewest Negroes 15 to 19 years of age for whom any secondary work is offered. The Negro population 15 to 19 years of age is 10.9 per cent of the total Negro population of the State of Tennessee.

Appendix

TABLE 30

PUBLIC SECONDARY SCHOOLS FOR NEGROES IN TEXAS SHOWN ACCORDING TO NUMBER OF SCHOOLS AND COUNTIES OFFERING 0 TO 4 YEARS OF WORK, 1932-33

Number of Years of Work Offered	Number of Schools			Counties Offering		Per Cent of Negro Population of State, 15 to 19 years living in Counties Offering
	Urban	Rural	Total	Number	Population 15 to 19 years of age	
0 years				121†	1,361*	1.4
1 year only	12	74	86	9	512	.5
2 years only	11	106	117	16	2,167	2.2
3 years only	21	98	119	27	8,418	9.0
4 years	76	46	122	78	80,238	86.9
Total	120	324	444	254	92,696	100.0

† Data on Tyler (286), Refugio (98), and Rockwell (216) counties not available.

* Of this number, 1,066 are distributed among 117 Counties having less than 50 Negroes 15 to 19 years of age.

TABLE 31

ENROLLMENT AND NUMBER OF TEACHERS BY YEARS OF WORK OFFERED IN PUBLIC SECONDARY SCHOOLS FOR NEGROES IN TEXAS, 1932-33

Schools Offering	Enrollment							Number of Teachers		
	Years of Work Offered				Total	Urban	Rural	In Accredited Schools	Full Time	Part Time	Total
	I	II	III	IV							
1 year only	787				787	354	433		21	83	104
2 years only	719	603			1,322	197	1,125		36	91	127
3 years only	1,155	846	699		2,700	581	2,119		87	83	170
4 years	5,570	4,675	3,727	3,800	17,772	15,408	2,364	11,032*	572	94	666
Total	8,231	6,124	4,426	3,800	22,581	16,540	6,041	11,032	716	351	1,067

* There are 35 accredited 4 year secondary schools included in this study. (Accredited schools for 1931-32).

TEXAS

(1932-1933)

PUBLIC SECONDARY SCHOOL WORK OFFERED IN COUNTIES

None: (121)

County	#	County	#	County	#
Andrews (E)	0	Gillespie (C)	10	Moore (Nw)	0
Aransas (S)	1	Glasscock (W)	2	Motley (Nw)	32
Archer (N)	1	Gray (Nw)	23	Nolan (Nw)	59
Armstrong (Nw)	1	Hale (Nw)	21	Ochiltree (Nw)	0
		Hall (Nw)	76	Oldham (Nw)	0
Atascosa (S)	24	Hamilton (C)	0	Parmer (Nw)	0
Bailey (Nw)	2	Hansford (N)	0	Pecos (W)	4
Bandera (Sw)	1	Hartley (Nw)	0	Presidio (W)	3
Baylor (N)	1	Haskell (N)	39	Randall (Nw)	2
Borden (Nw)	0	Hemphill (Nw)	2	Reagan (W)	0
Brewster (W)	7	Hidalgo (S)	32	Real (Sw)	0
Briscoe (Nw)	10	Hockley (Nw)	11	Reeves (W)	16
Brooks (S)	1	Hood (N)	12	Roberts (Nw)	0
Callahan (N)	3	Howard (Nw)	34	San Patricio (S)	36
Carson (Nw)	0	Hudspeth (W)	1		
Castro (Nw)	0	Hutchinson (Nw)	6	Schleicher (W)	3
Clay (N)	32			Scurry (Nw)	9
Cochran (Nw)	1	Irion (W)	0	Schackelford (N)	23
Coke (W)	4	Jeff Davis (W)	1		
Collingsworth (Nw)	87	Jim Hogg (S)	4	Sherman (Nw)	0
		Jim Wells (S)	33	Somervell (N)	0
Comal (C)	26	Kendall (C)	5	Starr (S)	0
Comanche (C)	0	Kenedy (S)	0	Sterling (W)	0
Concho (C)	7	Kent (Nw)	2	Stonewall (Nw)	30
Crane (W)	3	Kerr (Sw)	39	Sutton (W)	4
Crockett (W)	1	Kimble (C)	1	Swicher (Nw)	3
Crosby (Nw)	23	King (Nw)	7	Terrell (W)	1
Colberson (W)	0	Kinney (Sw)	41	Terry (Nw)	8
Dallam (Nw)	0	Knox (N)	25	Throckmorton (N)	1
Dawson (Nw)	16	Lamb (Nw)	24		
Dimmit (Sw)	1	LaSalle (S)	8	ValVerde (W)	25
Donley (Nw)	18	Lipscomb (Nw)	0	Ward (W)	8
Duval (S)	2	Live Oak (S)	13	Webb (S)	10
Ector (W)	10	Liano (C)	7	Wheeler (Nw)	26
Edwards (W)	1	Loving (W)	0	Willacy (S)	12
Fisher (Ne)	40	Martin (Nw)	6	Wilson (S)	73
Floyd (Nw)	9	Mason (C)	16	Winkler (W)	17
Foard (N)	32	Maverick (Sw)	2	Wise (N)	12
Frio (Sw)	12	McMullen (S)	2	Yoakum (Nw)	0
Gaines (Nw)	0	Menard (C)	19	Young (N)	16
Garza (Nw)	3	Midland (W)	19	Zapata (Sw)	0
Deaf Smith (Nw)	1	Mills (C)	0	Zavala (Sw)	3
		Montague (N)	1		

1 Year Only: (9)

County	#	County	#	County	#
Cameron (S)	72	Franklin (Ne)	59	Rains (Ne)	86
Childress (Nw)	66	Hardman (N)	59	Runnels (C)	66
Eastland (W)	62	Lynn (Nw)	24	Upton (W)	18

Appendix

2 Years Only: (16)

Blanco (C)	10	Fannin (Ne)	506	San Saba (C)	19
Bosque (C)	72	Karnes (S)	132	Stephens (N)	40
Burnet (C)	10	Matagorda (Se)	504	Uvalde (Sw)	40
Coleman (C)	66	McCulloch (C)	42	Wood (Ne)	538
Delta (Ne)	121	Medina (Sw)	27		
Erath (N)	15	Parker (N)	25		

3 Years Only: (26)

Austin (Se)	588	Hunt (Ne)	684	Nueces (S)	231
Bee (S)	77	Jack (N)	6	Palo Pinto (N)	107
Brazoria (Se)	824	Jackson (Se)	224	Polk (E)	670
Calhoun (S)	69	Jones (N)	68	Sabine (E)	236
Chambers (Se)	137	Kleberg (S)	48	San Jacinto (E)	638
Cottle (Nw)	54	Lampasas (C)	25	Upshur (Ne)	879
Denton (N)	227	Leon (E)	1,038	Van Zandt (Ne)	281
Dickens (Nw)	45	Madison (E)	415	Wilbarger (N)	163
Goliad (S)	112	Mitchell (Nw)	83		

4 Years, But No Accredited School: (50)

Anderson (E)	1,342	Hays (C)	2,402	Potter (Nw)	131
Angelina (E)	427	Henderson (Ne)	704	Red River (Ne)	924
Brazos (C)	1,017	Hill (C)	656	Robertson (C)	1,236
Brown (C)	102	Hopkins (Ne)	364	Rusk (Ne)	1,603
Burleson (C)	753	Houston (E)*	1,588	San Augustin	
Caldwell (C)	527	Johnson (N)	206	(E)	478
Cass (Ne)*	1,362	Kaufman (Ne)	1,397	Shelby (E)	857
Collin (Ne)	475	Lavaca (Se)	397	Smith (Ne)	2,381
Colorado (Se)	634	Lee (C)	507	Taylor (N)	310
Cooke (W)	130	Liberty (Se)*	548	Titus (Ne)	366
Coryell (C)	160	Lubbock (Nw)	162	Tom Green (W)	109
Ellis (Ne)	1,558	Marion (Ne)	776	Trinity (E)	387
Freestone (E)	1,034	Montgomery		Victoria (S)	316
Gonzales (S)	745	(Se)	570	Walker (E)	1,008
Grimes (E)	1,204	Morris (Ne)	489	Waller (Se)	590
Guadalupe (S)*	530	Nacodoches (E)	887	Wharton (Se)	879
Hardin (E)	237	Newton (E)	510		
Harrison (Ne)*	3,614	Panola (Ne)	1,297		

Counties Having One Accredited Public Secondary School, or More: (28)

Bastrop (C)	811	Fort Bend (Se)	922	Milam (C)	1,020
Bell (C)	727	Galveston (Se)	1,153	Navarro (Ne)	1,662
Bexar (S)	1,022	Grayson (Ne)	759	Orange (E)	276
Bowie (Ne)	1,003	Gregg (Ne)	997	Tarrant (N)	2,054
Camp (Ne)	515	Harris (Se)	6,284	Travis (C)	1,108
Cherokee (E)	1,417	Jasper (E)	563	Washington (Se)	1,208
Dallas (Ne)	4,083	Jefferson (Se)	3,147	Wichita (N)	412
DeWitt (S)	469	Lamar (Ne)	1,118	Williamson (C)	814
El Paso (W)	123	Limestone (C)	1,318		
Falls (C)	1,434	McLennan (C)	2,060		

* One school in each county had been accredited by May 7, 1934, according to Mr. D. B. Taylor of the Division of Negro Education.

Notes: Data not available for Tyler (296), Refugio, (98) and Rockwell (216) Counties. Jack County (6) has the fewest Negroes 15 to 19 years of age for whom any secondary work is offered. The Negro Population 15 to 19 years of age is 10.8 per cent of the total Negro population of the State of Texas.

TABLE 32

Public Secondary Schools for Negroes in Virginia Shown According to Number of Schools and Counties Offering 0 to 4 Years of Work, 1932-33

Number of Years of Work Offered	Number of Schools			Counties Offering		Per Cent of Negro Population of State, 15 to 19 years living in Counties Offering
	Urban	Rural	Total	Number	Population 15 to 19 years of age	
0 years				28	5,684*	7.7
1 year only	0	5	5	2	1,895	2.6
2 years only	4	11	15	5	2,183	2.9
3 years only	1	16	17	13	4,972	6.8
4 years	14	48	62	52	58,709	80.0
Total	19	80	99	100	73,443	100.0

* Of this number, 335 are distributed among 10 Counties having less than 50 Negroes 15 to 19 years of age.

TABLE 33

Enrollment and Number of Teachers by Years of Work Offered in Public Secondary Schools for Negroes in Virginia, 1932-33

Schools Offering	Enrollment							Number of Teachers		
	Years of Work Offered				Total	Urban	Rural	In Accredited Schools	Full Time	Part Time	Total
	I	II	III	IV							
1 year only	121				121	0	121		3	2	5
2 years only	302	169			471	170	301		19	5	24
3 years only	265	212	140		617	67	550		29	9	38
4 years	3,924	2,710	2,077	1,510	10,221	6,758	3,463	9,687*	363	46	409
Total	4,612	3,091	2,217	1,510	11,430	6,995	4,435	9,687	414	62	476

* There are 33 accredited 4 year secondary schools included in this study.

Appendix 161

VIRGINIA
(1932-1933)
PUBLIC SECONDARY SCHOOL WORK OFFERED IN COUNTIES

None: (28)

Bland(Sw)	17	Greene (E)	145	Princess Anne	
Buchanan (Sw)	7	Giles (Sw)	67	(Se)	926
Carroll (Sw)	47	Henry (S)	793	Rappahannock	
Craig (W)	0	Highland (Nw)	13	(N)	225
Dickinson (Sw)	18	King George(S)	204	Richmond (E)	369
Essex (E)	461	Lee(Sw)	50	Russell (Cw)	66
Fairfax (N)	497	Madison (N)	284	Scott (Sw)	34
Floyd (Sw)	68	Nelson (C)	532	Shenandoah (N)	49
Fluvanna (C)	231	Page (N)	81	Stafford (Ne)	164
Grayson (Sw)	90	Patrick (S)	164	Warren (N)	82

1 Year Only: (2)

Amelia (C)	570	Northampton (E)	1,325

2 Years Only: (5)

Bath (W)	117	Culpeper (N)	487	Pulaski (W)	224
Botetourt (W)	251	Louisa (C)	667		

3 Years Only: (13)

Accomac (E)	1,679	Loudoun (N)	493	Westmoreland (Ne)	502
Amherst (W)	665	Mathews (E)	235	Wythe (Sw)	161
Arlington (N)	280	New Kent (E)	315		
Frederick (N)	166	Orange (C)	408		
King William (E)	484	Rockbridge (W)	231		
		Sussex (Se)	1,034		

4 Years, But No Accredited School in County: (20)

Alleghany (W)	322	Hanover (E)	1,063	Tazewell (Sw)	248
Appomattox (C)	301	King and Queen (E)	501	Wise (Sw)	267
Brunswick (S)*	1,522			York (Se)	336
Buckingham (C)	701	Powhatan (C)	380	Southampton	2,023
Clarke (N)	183	Prince George (Se)	505	Spotsylvania	368
Fauquier (N)	688			Washington	170
Franklin (S)	488	Smyth (Sw)	89		
Goochland (C)	520	Surry (Se)	527		

* The St. Paul N. and I. School in Lawrenceville, Brunswick County, provides only 4-year secondary work in the county.

Counties Having One Four-Year Accredited Secondary School, or More: (32)

Albemarle (C)....	668	Greenville (S)....	990	Northumberland (E)	542
Augusta (Nw)....	391	Halifax (S)........	2,435	Nottoway (S)....	825
Bedford (W)......	882	Henrico (E).......	721	Pittsylvania (S)	563
Campbell (S)......	841	Isle of Wight (Se).................	799	Prince Edward (S)	957
Caroline (Ne)....	945	James City (Se)	359		
Charles City (Se)	462	Lancaster (E)....	468	Prince William* (N)	302
Charlotte (S)......	787	Lunenburg (S)..	753	Roanoke (S)........	1,280
Chesterfield (C)..	1,115	Mecklenburg (S)	2,227	Warwick (Se)....	1,531
Cumberland (C)	514	Montgomery (Sw)*	242	Middlesex (S)....	573
Dinwiddie (S)....	1,270	Nansemond (S)..	1,885	Rockingham (Nw)	178
Elizabeth City (Se)	721	Norfolk (Se)......	1,450		
Gloucester (E)..	576				

* Private schools which provide secondary work for Negro educables of the county, and are paid tuition fees by public authorities.

The following cities provide secondary facilities for educables from county districts:

Clifton Forge (Alleghany), Fredericksburg (Spottsylvania), Winchester (Frederick), Williamsburg (James City), Harrisonburg (Rockingham), and Newport News (Warwick).

Notes: Frederick County (53) has the fewest Negroes 15 to 19 years of age for whom secondary work is offered. The Negro population 15 to 19 years of age is 11.3 per cent of the total Negro population of the State of Virginia.

TABLE 34

PUBLIC SECONDARY SCHOOLS FOR NEGROES OF WEST VIRGINIA SHOWN ACCORDING TO NUMBER OF SCHOOLS AND COUNTIES OFFERING 0 TO 4 YEARS OF WORK, 1932-33

Number of Years of Work Offered	Number of Schools			Counties Offering		Per Cent of Negro Population of State, 15 to 19 years living in Counties Offering
	Urban	Rural	Total	Number	Population 15 to 19 years of age	
0 years				32	685*	6.9
1 year only	3	5	8	1	225	2.2
2 years only		4	4	2	149	1.5
3 years only						
4 years	15	14	29	20	9,050	89.4
Total	18	23	41	55	10,109	100.0

* Of this number 228 are distributed among 26 counties having less than 50 Negroes 15 to 19 years of age.

TABLE 35

ENROLLMENT AND NUMBER OF TEACHERS BY YEARS OF WORK OFFERED IN PUBLIC SECONDARY SCHOOLS FOR NEGROES IN WEST VIRGINIA, 1932-33

Schools Offering	Enrollment							Number of Teachers		
	Years of Work Offered				Total	Urban	Rural	In Accredited Schools	Full Time	Part Time	Total
	I	II	III	IV							
1 year only	411*				411*	227	184		8	19	27
2 years only	31	24			55		55		4	2	6
3 years only											
4 years	1,029	1,021	737	617	3,404	1,846	1,558	2,948	196	20	216
Total	1,471	1,045	737	617	3,870	2,073	1,797	2,948ᵃ	208	41	249

*Of this number, all enrolled in the 9th grade of the junior high school at Charleston.
ᵃ There are 20 accredited 4 year secondary schools included in this study.

WEST VIRGINIA
(1932-1933)
PUBLIC SECONDARY SCHOOL WORK OFFERED IN COUNTIES

None: (32)

Barbour (N)	118	Lewis (C)	9	Preston (Ne)	3
Braxton (C)	20	Lincoln (W)	2	Putnam (W)	12
Brooke (N)	80	Marshall (Ne)	33	Ritchie (Nw)	1
Calhoun (C)	1	Mason (W)	79	Roane (Nw)	0
Clay (C)	6	Mineral (Ne)	54	Tucker (Ne)	9
Doddridge (N)	3	Monroe (Se)	58	Tyler (N)	5
Gilmer (C)	3	Morgan (Ne)	10	Wayne (W)	16
Grant (Ne)	30	Nicholas (C)	3	Webster (C)	0
Hampshire (Ne)	7	Pendleton (E)	9	Wetzel (N)	5
Hardy (Ne)	36	Pleasants (Nw)	0	Wirt (Nw)	0
Jackson (Nw)	1	Pocohontas (E)	68		

1 Year Only: (1)

Greenbrier (Se)... 225

2 Years Only: (2)

Boone (Sw)........ 75   Taylor (N).......... 74

3 Years Only: (0)

4 Years, But No Accredited Secondary Schools: (8)

Berkeley (Ne)	174	Ohio (N)	194	Upshur* (C)	16
Hancock (N)	79	Randolph (E)	45	Wyoming (S)	175
Manongahelia (N)	164	Summers (S)	112		

Counties Having One Accredited Secondary School, or More: (12)

Cabell (W)	393	Kenawha (W)	1,333	Mercer (S)	759
Fayette (C)	1,103	Logan (Sw)	491	Mingo (Sw)	262
Harrison (N)	195	Marion (N)	317	Raleigh (S)	971
Jefferson (Ne)	265	McDowell (S)	1,944	Wood (Nw)	50

* Upshur County (16) has the fewest Negroes 15 to 19 years of age for whom any secondary work is offered.

Note: The Negro population 15 to 19 years of age is 8.8 per cent of the total Negro population of the State of West Virginia.

APPENDIX D*

TABLE 1

ENROLLMENT AND NUMBER OF TEACHERS IN SCHOOLS AIDED BY THE SLATER FUND AS COUNTY TRAINING SCHOOLS IN WHICH 1 YEAR OF SECONDARY WORK WAS OFFERED IN 1933

State	Number of Schools			Secondary Enrollment			Number of Secondary Teachers		
	Rural	Urban	Total	Rural	Urban	Total	Full Time	Part Time	Total
Alabama	1		1	6		6		1	1
Arkansas	7	2	9	87	56	143	6	10	16
Florida	1	1	2	1		1		1	1
Georgia	4	1	5	57	23	80	4	2	6
Louisiana	1	1	2	14	12	26	2		2
Mississippi	2		2	23		23	1	1	2
N. Carolina	1		1	10		10		1	1
S. Carolina	4	1	5	23	24	47	2	6	8
Texas	2		2	11		11		2	2
Virginia	2		2	40		40	1	1	2
	25	6	31	272	115	387	16	25	41

Note: Kentucky, Maryland, Missouri, Oklahoma and Tennessee had no County Training Schools offering only 1 year of secondary work.

TABLE 2

ENROLLMENT AND NUMBER OF TEACHERS IN SCHOOLS AIDED BY THE SLATER FUND AS COUNTY TRAINING SCHOOLS IN WHICH 2 YEARS OF SECONDARY WORK WAS OFFERED IN 1933

State	Number of Schools			Secondary Enrollment			Number of Secondary Teachers		
	Rural	Urban	Total	Rural	Urban	Total	Full Time	Part Time	Total
Alabama	3	1	4	41	72	113	3	5	8
Arkansas	6	5	11	105	149	254	14	13	27
Florida	5	2	7	84	31	115	9	8	17
Georgia	13	6	19	269	258	527	18	21	39
Kentucky	7	1	8	111	16	127	8	3	11
Mississippi	18	2	20	387	44	431	26	17	43
N. Carolina	1	1	2	35	18	53	2		2
Oklahoma	1		1	12		12		1	1
S. Carolina	7	1	8	154	65	219	6	10	16
Tennessee	3	2	5	95	43	138	5	2	7
Texas	1		1	16		16		1	1
Virginia	7	1	8	124	94	218	10	4	14
	72	22	94	1,433	790	2,223	101	85	186

Note: Maryland, Missouri, and Louisiana had no County Training Schools offering only 2 years of secondary work.

*All data presented in this appendix were collected and compiled by the author.

TABLE 3

Enrollment and Number of Teachers in Schools Aided by the Slater Fund as County Training Schools in Which 3 Years of Secondary Work Was Offered in 1933

State	Number of Schools			Secondary Enrollment			Number of Secondary Teachers		
	Rural	Urban	Total	Rural	Urban	Total	Full Time	Part Time	Total
Alabama	3		3	77		77	5	1	6
Arkansas	4	2	6	158	96	254	12	8	20
Georgia	6	1	7	192	67	259	12	3	15
Kentucky	4	1	5	67	33	100	5	5	10
Louisiana	2	1	3	34	32	66	5	4	9
Mississippi	4	6	10	131	397	528	19	8	27
N. Carolina	4	1	5	112	180	292	5	4	9
Oklahoma	1		1	38		38	4		4
S. Carolina	16	3	19	833	364	1,197	40	9	49
Tennessee	1	3	4	54	191	245	11	1	12
Texas	9	2	11	262	86	348	14	7	21
Virginia	13	1	14	498	42	540	25	6	31
	67	21	88	2,456	1,488	3,944	157	56	213

Note: Maryland and Missouri had no County Training Schools offering only 3 years of secondary work.

TABLE 4

Enrollment and Number of Teachers in Schools Aided by the Slater Fund as County Training Schools in Which 4 Years of Secondary Work Was Offered in 1933

State	Number of Schools			Secondary Enrollment			Number of Secondary Teachers		
	Rural	Urban	Total	Rural	Urban	Total	Full Time	Part Time	Total
Alabama	35	1	36	2,231	94	2,325	111	50	161
Arkansas	2	8	10	218	923	1,141	44	9	53
Florida		44	14	1,913		1,913	66	19	85
Georgia	20	13	33	1,397	1,354	2,751	107	24	131
Kentucky	11	20	31	450	1,305	1,755	97	7	104
Louisiana	13	19	32	727	1,335	2,062	103	35	138
Maryland	1	1	2	143	107	250	5	4	9
Mississippi	11	11	22	1,064	1,389	2,453	91	16	107
Missouri	1	2	3	49	50	99	7	1	8
N. Carolina	44	27	71	5,637	3,972	9,609	311	16	327
Oklahoma	6	3	9	526	290	816	34	7	41
S. Carolina	13	14	27	855	2,221	3,076	109	12	121
Tennessee	10	15	25	700	3,415	4,115	134	17	151
Texas	22	18	40	1,167	2,914	4,081	147	18	165
Virginia	41	3	44	3,196	222	3,418	142	21	163
	230	169	399	20,273	19,591	39,864	1,508	256	1,764

APPENDIX E

TABLE

DISBURSEMENTS MADE TO PUBLIC NEGRO SECONDARY SCHOOLS IN 15 SOUTHERN STATES THROUGH THE JOHN F. SLATER FUND, 1911-1933

Year	Alabama	Arkansas	Florida	Georgia	Kentucky	Louisiana	Maryland	Mississippi
1911-12	$	$ 500.00	$	$	$	$ 1,000.00	$	$ 500.00
1912-13	....	500.00	....	500.00	....	1,000.00	....	....
1913-14	500.00	500.00	....	1,000.00	500.00	1,000.00	....	1,000.00
1914-15	500.00	1,000.00	....	1,300.00	500.00	2,000.00	....	90.26
1915-16	3,500.00	2,250.00	....	1,905.00	870.00	870.00	....	870.00
1916-17	3,000.00	1,740.00	....	2,531.00	1,432.00	1,332.00	....	1,432.00
1917-18	3,788.00	2,430.00	....	2,764.00	1,132.00	2,066.00	500.00	1,865.00
1918-19	6,462.00	2,664.00	500.00	4,500.00	2,000.00	3,334.00	1,000.00	2,000.00
1919-20	7,500.00	3,000.00	500.00	5,000.00	3,500.00	4,500.00	500.00	4,750.00
1920-21	6,600.00	2,850.00	500.00	4,750.00	3,700.00	4,250.00	200.00	5,200.00
1921-22	5,850.00	3,700.00	....	5,600.00	3,500.00	4,550.00	200.00	6,150.00
1922-23	5,900.00	3,700.00	900.00	6,600.00	3,700.00	5,400.00	200.00	7,350.00
1923-24	7,000.00	4,450.00	1,800.00	7,150.00	4,250.00	4,450.00	200.00	7,900.00
1924-25	7,500.00	4,350.00	2,300.00	8,800.00	4,750.00	6,200.00	200.00	10,900.00
1925-26	10,050.00	5,800.00	2,800.00	9,300.00	5,350.00	6,600.00	200.00	11,250.00
1926-27	11,500.00	5,900.00	3,800.00	9,100.00	6,000.00	6,500.00	200.00	11,000.00
1927-28	10,200.00	5,875.00	3,600.00	17,886.96	5,450.00	10,481.99	....	16,500.00
1928-29	15,000.00	9,700.00	6,000.00	15,658.91	5,500.00	9,135.00	....	14,355.00
1929-30	13,050.00	8,439.00	5,220.00	12,610.46	4,785.00	8,100.00	....	12,400.00
1930-31	11,223.00	7,285.00	4,350.00	10,850.00	3,975.00	6,100.00	....	9,775.00
1931-32	8,750.00	5,750.00	4,050.00	9,250.00	3,100.00	5,100.00	....	8,175.00
1932-33	7,365.00	5,600.00	2,240.00		2,550.00			
Total	$145,238.00	$87,983.00	$38,560.00	$137,056.33	$62,844.00	$94,968.99	$3,400.00	$133,962.26

Compiled from original data in the office of the John F. Slater Fund, Washington, D. C., by the author.

(Table continued on page 168.)

TABLE

DISBURSEMENTS MADE TO PUBLIC NEGRO SECONDARY SCHOOLS IN 15 SOUTHERN STATES THROUGH THE JOHN F. SLATER FUND, 1911-1933

Year	Missouri	Oklahoma	Tennessee	N. Carolina	S. Carolina	Texas	Virginia	Total
1911-12	$	$	$	$	$	$	$	$ 2,000.00
1912-13	....	....	....	....	....	....	....	2,000.00
1913-14	....	....	....	....	....	....	....	4,000.00
1914-15	....	....	....	1,500.00	....	....	500.00	8,090.26
1915-16	....	....	2,000.00	3,800.00	500.00	500.00	1,500.00	18,350.00
1916-17	....	....	1,740.00	3,980.00	500.00	500.00	2,000.00	19,760.00
1917-18	....	....	2,430.00	4,760.00	870.00	1,305.00	2,610.00	27,190.00
1918-19	....	....	3,330.00	7,594.00	1,866.00	2,195.00	2,994.00	39,038.00
1919-20	....	....	4,500.00	9,500.00	3,264.00	2,500.00	4,397.00	52,893.00
1920-21	....	500.00	4,450.00	8,700.00	4,500.00	3,060.00	7,499.00	62,400.00
1921-22	....	1,000.00	5,050.00	7,100.00	5,600.00	4,350.00	10,600.00	62,050.00
1922-23	....	2,000.00	5,100.00	8,200.00	6,500.00	4,950.00	9,800.00	66,800.00
1923-24	....	2,000.00	5,300.00	7,250.00	6,300.00	4,950.00	9,750.00	72,900.00
1924-25	....	2,000.00	5,400.00	8,000.00	6,500.00	4,750.00	10,050.00	75,600.00
1925-26	....	2,475.00	6,300.00	12,750.00	7,000.00	4,500.00	10,100.00	102,275.00
1926-27	....	2,350.00	6,800.00	13,250.00	10,400.00	6,000.00	14,250.00	110,800.00
1927-28	....	2,000.00	6,550.00	12,500.00	12,400.00	6,800.00	14,650.00	106,475.00
1928-29	....	2,500.00	8,500.00	15,000.00	12,000.00	7,100.00	14,400.00	149,868.95
1929-30	....	2,175.00	7,395.00	13,075.00	18,500.00	8,000.00	16,300.00	130,523.91
1930-31	500.00	1,800.00	6,650.00	11,375.00	16,095.00	6,960.00	14,181.00	111,893.46
1931-32	500.00	1,400.00	5,200.00	8,500.00	13,575.00	5,800.00	12,250.00	88,825.00
1932-33	1,000.00	1,200.00	4,500.00	6,800.00	10,950.00	4,500.00	9,500.00	75,280.00
Total	$2,000.00	$23,400.00	$91,195.00	$163,634.00	$146,520.00	$82,520.00	$175,831.00	$1,389,112.58

VITA

Edward Redcay. Born, October 13, 1902, in Philadelphia, Pennsylvania.

Academic Training: Dartmouth College, 1927, B.S.; Yale University, 1929-30 (part-time); Michigan University, Summer 1930; Dartmouth College, 1931, M.A.; Yale University, 1932-33.

Scholarships: Yale University, 1932-33.

Honors: Honors in Education, Dartmouth College.

Professonal Experience: 1927-1928-1929-1930, The Roxbury School, Cheshire, Conn., Instructor in Biological Sciences and Coach.

1930-1931, Dartmouth College, Hanover, N. H., Instructor in History of Education and Educational Administration.

1931-32, Elm City School, New Haven, Conn., Special Lecturer in Zoology.

1933- The Anna T. Jeanes Foundation and the John F. Slater Fund, Washington, D. C., Special Research Agent.

Member: Kappa Phi Kappa, National Education Association, The American Country Life Association, and the Progressive Education Association.